Journeys toward Narrative Preaching

Journeys toward Narrative Preaching

Edited by WAYNE BRADLEY ROBINSON

THE PILGRIM PRESS
NEW YORK

Biblical quotations, unless otherwise noted, are from the Revised Standard Version of the Bible, copyright 1946, 1952, © 1971, 1973 by the Division of Christian Education of the National Council of the Churches of Christ in the U.S.A., and are used by permission.

Book design by Publishers' WorkGroup

Library of Congress Cataloging-in-Publication Data
Journeys toward narrative preaching / edited by Wayne Bradley
  Robinson
     p.   cm.
Includes bibliographical references.
ISBN 0-8298-0832-9
  1. Preaching.   2. Storytelling—Religious aspects—Christianity.
I. Robinson, Wayne Bradley, 1936- .
BV4235.S76J68   1990
251—dc20   89-36683
                                                      CIP

The Pilgrim Press, 475 Riverside Drive, New York, NY 10115

Contents

CONTENTS

Contributors

ROBERT G. HUGHES, St. John's Professor of Practical Theology, Lutheran Theological School, Philadelphia, Pennsylvania

EUGENE L. LOWRY, William K. McElvaney Professor of Preaching, St. Paul School of Theology, Kansas City, Missouri

WAYNE BRADLEY ROBINSON, Adjunct Professor of Preaching, United Theological Seminary of the Twin Cities, New Brighton, Minnesota

LUCY ROSE, Assistant Professor of Worship and Preaching, Columbia Theological Seminary, Decatur, Georgia

RICHARD L. THULIN, Ulrich Professor of the Art of Preaching, Lutheran Theological Seminary, Gettysburg, Pennsylvania

MICHAEL E. WILLIAMS, Director of Preaching Ministries, Section on Worship, United Methodist General Board of Discipleship

Journeys toward Narrative Preaching

Journeys toward Narrative Preaching

WAYNE BRADLEY ROBINSON

This volume is the outcome of the work of six members of the Narrative and Imagination working group of the Academy of Homiletics. The academy's overall purpose is to "bring together professors and teachers of homiletics for the study of the place of preaching in theological education, for the discussion and sharing of ideas and methods, and for the fostering of scholarly research in this and other related areas and disciplines."[1] The working groups gather to give special focus to this purpose.

We hope that this volume will encourage those who have not tried narrative preaching to do so, especially since we present a variety of models of how to do narrative preaching and show how each of us moved toward the particular model we present. We also hope that this volume will contribute to the development of the discipline of narrative preaching. Before going into the specifics about this particular project, it is important that we address some broader issues related to narrative, in particular to narrative preaching.

Many people wonder why there is so much interest in narrative. Is it simply the latest fad or are there deeper reasons? For all of us involved in this project, narrative preaching is not just the latest trend. We share a commitment to it as a way to do preaching, a way that has the potential to be one of the ways, if not the most

1

impactful way, to faithfully carry out the homiletical task. When done well, narrative preaching has the power to effect the kind of transformation in people's lives which we all hope for when we as vehicles attempt to communicate the good news.

This is so in part because narrative preaching both reflects and impacts on the narrative quality of life as we live it. We recognize ourselves in narratives, and we can imagine ourselves changed through narrative in a way that does not often happen through other means of preaching. Although Fred Craddock is speaking about the inductive pattern of communicating as opposed to the deductive, his words could also apply to narrative when he says: "Everyone lives inductively, not deductively. No farmer deals with the problem of calfhood, only with the calf. The woman in the kitchen is not occupied with the culinary arts in general but with a particular roast or cake. The wood craftsman is hardly able to discuss intelligently the topic of 'chairness,' but he is a master with a chair. . . . The minister says 'all [people] are mortal' and meets with drowsy agreement; [s]he announces that 'Mr. Brown's son is dying' and the church becomes the church."[2]

Craddock's point about life as we live it in its "everydayness" leads him, not coincidentally, to a point about the life of faith. Indeed, this leads us to another reason why narrative preaching is so fitting for the expression of the good news in sermonic form: The life of faith has a narrative quality about it. We see this in the Bible, which is grounded in narrative. In the heart of the Hebrew Scripture, we hear the instructions that when the people come into the sanctuary to present their offerings, they are to say:

> A wandering Aramean was my father; and he went down into Egypt and sojourned there, few in number; and there he became a nation, great, mighty, and populous. And the Egyptians treated us harshly, and afflicted us, and laid upon us hard bondage. Then we cried to the Lord the God of our fathers, and the Lord heard our voice and saw our affliction, our toil and our oppression; and the Lord brought us out of Egypt with a mighty hand and an outstretched arm, with great terror, with signs and wonders; and God brought us to this place and gave us this land, a land flowing with milk and honey. (Deut. 26:5–9)

The core of Christian Scripture has the same quality as that of Hebrew Scripture. It is the narrative of the birth, life, death, and resurrection of Jesus whom we confess to be the Christ. And our own faith pilgrimage has an echoing narrative quality about it as we move from baptism to death to resurrection with Jesus. It is also worth noting how much Jesus used narrative forms for his own preaching; so it seems worthwhile to attend not just to his ideas but to the form in which those ideas were communicated.

The narrative quality of the life of faith shows up in other areas as well. Worship at its best has a narrative flow to it. Take the worship design based on the call of Isaiah as an example. It moves from adoration ("I saw the Lord sitting upon a throne high and lifted up") or opening equilibrium, to confession ("Woe is me for I am lost") or disequilibrium, to escalation ("and I dwell in the midst of a people of unclean lips"), to forgiveness ("Then flew one of the seraphim . . . and he said . . . , 'Your guilt is taken away, your sin forgiven' ") or reversal, to challenge and response ("Whom shall I send," "Here am I, send me") or closing denouement. This is a classic narrative framework. Within this narrative framework for worship, narrative preaching seems especially fitting.

In addition, the church year and the Scripture readings geared to its framework also have a narrative quality to them. In the liturgical year, we move from the anticipation of the birth of Jesus, to the birth, to the spread of the good news of his birth, to his baptism and temptations, to his ministry, to his crucifixion and resurrection, to the expansion of the early church. With this narrative framework, along with the model of Jesus' own preaching, it hardly seems that narrative is something that has just sprung up and will soon fade away like some cultural fad. We may be rediscovering narrative as a major mode for preaching, but it is hardly a new phenomenon.

By looking at the Isaiah model for worship, we have already begun to look at another important issue regarding narrative. Although the Isaiah text is the "story" of his call, the underlying narrative framework has been extracted from it and used as a model for worship. For many people, the terms *narrative* and *story* are virtually synonymous,[3] which leads many to react with some skepticism about narrative. They either cannot envision themselves as storytellers or they associate story with make-believe, fiction, and therefore not suited to the serious issues of faith.

This association of story with make-believe is unfortunate because story is much more than make-believe. If we look at the word *story*, we see that it is a much richer word than is often thought. The word *story* comes from the same root as does *history*, and at one time meant exactly the same thing. But even today, Webster's first two definitions of *story* (after "history") are: "an account of incidents or events; a statement regarding the facts pertinent to a situation in question." It is not until the seventh definition that the negative connotations of "lie and falsehood" appear. Then the last definition is simply "a news article or broadcast."[4] So even the word *story* has a range of uses that suggest the story's place in preaching. I agree, however, with Eugene Lowry that we would be best served by keeping the terms *story* and *narrative* separate and defining them differently for the purpose of their use in homiletics. He says: "The term *story*—as I am suggesting here—is quite restricted in breadth. It refers to a tale drawn from any number of numerous literary forms: myth, parable, saga, etc. By the term *narrative* I mean a particular shape that discourse might take. Although other models are possible, in my writings I have concentrated on one which bears a close resemblance to Aristotle's ideas expressed in *Poetics*. By *narrative sermon* I mean an event-in-time which moves from opening disequilibrium (or conflict) through escalation (complication) to surprising reversal (*peripetia*) into closing denouement."[5] It is worth noting how similar this framework is to the Isaiah text reference. But the main benefit of making such a distinction between narrative and story (although I would add to Lowry's sources for tales those tales drawn from life experience, which would have a somewhat different narrative flow) is that it frees us to use the narrative model even though we may not feel ready or inclined to do pure story-form preaching as it has been conventionally conceived. In short, a story sermon as defined by Lowry is always a narrative sermon, but not all narrative sermons are story sermons.

Having said that, it is still true that in the field of narrative preaching at this time there is no fixed understanding of what is and what is not narrative. For some, narrative does indeed mean the same thing as story as we have defined it here. For others, it is a much broader and more elastic category. In any case, it is in the nature of such a young discipline as narrative preaching for there to be so little agreement about its parameters. It seemed to us, then, that the variety we were bringing to the task would be an asset rather than a liability. It reminds me of the four Gospels, whose authors are in profound agreement about the core of what the faith narrative is but fulfill their task in rather different ways.

Similarly, we agree on the form in which we chose to present our various approaches. We have each written a *narrative* about how we individually came to conceive of the task of narrative preaching. We hope that this will encourage others to develop their own unique ways of doing narrative preaching. It also seemed fitting that a book about narrative should be itself in narrative form—the only one I know of where that is the case. We each include a sample sermon so that our readers can see how we use our own models. Please bear in mind, though, that these sermons are frozen-in-print versions of oral-aural events-in-time.

We hope that readers will enjoy discovering the extent to which our approaches to narrative preaching vary. For the purposes of this introduction, a few things about narrative perspective deserve mention. Our understandings of narrative range from that of Michael Williams, for whom narrative is practically synonymous with storytelling, to those of Eugene Lowry, Robert Hughes, Lucy Rose, and myself, for whom narrative is a pattern of development which can be used even though one might not tell a single story, to that of Richard Thulin, for whom the biblical narratives themselves are the major framework for narrative sermons.

In closing, I want to encourage you the reader to explore all the models presented here. Each author contributes to our understanding of narrative, whether you would choose to use his or her particular model or not. The six of us have all learned from one another as we have worked on this project and now offer these pieces as invitations to you to embark on or to go further on your own "journey toward narrative preaching."

NOTES

1. Constitution of the Academy of Homiletics.
2. Fred Craddock, *As One Without Authority* (Enid, Okla.: Phillips University Press, 1974), 60.

3. E.g., Michael Goldberg's book *Theology and Narrative: A Critical Introduction* (Nashville: Abingdon Press, 1981–82) appears to be about narrative, but most of the chapters are about story. Like many others, he uses the terms as synonyms.

4. *Webster's New Collegiate Dictionary*, 8th ed., s.v. "story."

5. Eugene Lowry, "The Difference Between Story Preaching and Narrative Preaching." Paper presented at the Academy of Homiletics Meeting, December, 1988, Drew University.

ONE

Retelling Biblical Narratives as the Foundation for Preaching

RICHARD L. THULIN

I have always been what one might call a narrative preacher. The biblical text has always been the central concern of my preaching. I want the biblical text to be given a voice and a hearing. I want its witness to the gracious work of God to be expressed in such a way that its offer and claim become real to those who speak and to those who listen. In attempting to live out this conviction, I have filled years of sermons with the retelling of stories recorded in both the Old and New Testaments. At times these stories have been updated, elaborated upon, furnished with a content, and interpreted. But the biblical stories themselves have lent my sermons shape, movement, and content. This has been true even when the preaching text has not been a story from one of the Testaments. Even non-narrative biblical texts are at least part of a story (Israel's or Paul's, for example). I have tended to preach such texts by telling that larger story without which the individual text has neither place nor definitive meaning. In such cases, again, the biblical stories have provided shape, movement, and context to the sermon.

A brief look through my files yields a sermon that I preached over twenty years ago. The biblical text was Exod. 14:21–31, the story of the Israelites crossing the Red Sea under Moses' leadership. An elaborate retelling of the crossing formed the major part of the sermon. I tried to picture the Israelites, an ill-organized, unarmed, panic-stricken conglomeration of men, women, and children, cowering at the water's edge. All had gone well until they reached the sea. I imagined that each step away from Egypt lightened their load and eased their fears. I even imagined them beginning to tell a few jokes, or at least laughing as they shared in the conversation of the free. Then they reached the sea and faced a trap worse than any nightmare could have conjured. On one side of them were the fortifications of Egypt. On another were the mountains. At their back was the fast-closing army of the Egyptians. And at their feet were the threatening waters of the sea. I tried to give voice to the despair expressed in Exod. 14:11: "Is it because there are no graves in Egypt that you have taken us away to die in the wilderness?" I also tried to picture the crossing itself: the command of the Lord which ordered the "people of Israel to go forward," the outstretched hand of Moses, water suddenly become dry ground, the pursuit, the mired chariots, the unsuccessful flight of the Egyptians, the deliverance, and the Israelites rejoicing, "Sing to the Lord, for God has triumphed gloriously."

Through this retelling I hoped that my listeners would identify with the seemingly trapped people of Israel. I wanted them to recognize themselves as people who despair of their own strength, as people who do not really anticipate an open future, and as people who find it difficult to trust in the God who orders them to stop complaining and move forward. Most of all, I wanted them to share the revelation that came to the Israelites on the far bank of the Red Sea: "The Lord is my strength and my song, and he has become my salvation." I wanted them to know that the God who called them and saved them is the sovereign Lord of human history. I wanted them, too, to believe and to step into life's threatening waters anticipating dry ground and final deliverance.

My files contain example after example of sermons that follow the basic shape of this sermon on Exodus 14. The biblical story is retold, with some elaboration of context and with some intensification of the human drama portrayed. The climax of the retelling is always a disclosure of the active God to whom we are invited to respond in faith. Such an invitation is made by direct address to those gathered to hear. Congregational engagement depends upon their identification with the human drama described. It also depends upon the naturalness with which the sermon's conclusions grow from the retold tale. The biblical story provides the shape, movement, and content.

My use of stories from other than biblical sources has often been quite different. I have used personal and communal stories, as well as stories from literature and a variety of public media. For the most part, however, these stories did not provide the shape, movement, and content of the sermon. They were used as illustrations, rather than as narratives, to explain or to dramatize or to provide an example of a central point. While they added color and vibrancy, in one sense they need not have been used at all. The main development of the sermons and their conclusions were quite clear without these stories. They highlighted key themes within the sermons, but they neither established nor advanced those themes.

Another sermon that I preached several years ago was entitled "The Ministry of Touch." It was based on Matt. 9:18–26, the story of the ailing woman who sought to touch Jesus' garment, told within the story of that ruler's dead daughter who "arose" when Jesus "took her by the hand." The sermon concluded with an invitation to a ministry of touch, a ministry that can be carried out before words are spoken, when words fail, or when words need additional confirmation. Four points that grew out of my study of the biblical text were developed as encouragement to the congregation to accept the invitation. I admitted that (1) it is a difficult thing to ask for help, even as (2) it is a difficult thing to be asked for help. Then I asserted that (3) our sense of the reality of others depends essentially upon touch, even as (4) does a sense of our own reality. I tried to demonstrate the accuracy of the first two points by referring to typical human occurrences. At times, for example, we find it difficult to ask for help because those around us deny the need. A friend in the hospital says, "I'm seriously ill," and those who visit say, "No, you're not." Likewise we find it difficult at times to be asked for help because any such request can place a heavy burden around our necks. The beggar on the street, the disabled car on the shoulder of the road, the friend who asks us to sell a block of raffle tickets for a favorite charity, each can cause unexpected interruption and inconvenience. I tried to demonstrate the accuracy of the last two points by telling two nonbiblical stories. I spoke about touch and the reality of the other by telling the story of our young son and his first encounter with a puppy. Simply looking at the dog was impossible. It had to be held and fingered and petted and squeezed. It was as though anything short of that would not certify the puppy's existence. I spoke about touch and a sense of our own reality by telling a brief fictionalized account of a person born without a sense of feeling. Her whole body "felt" like our arms do when we sleep on them for too long a time. She could not "pinch herself and see if she was awake." How could she tell whether she was asleep or awake, alive or dead?

My purpose in telling these stories was to further illustrate points already made in the sermon by reference to the biblical text. I did not want to depend solely upon the congregation's identification with the woman and girl of the biblical stories (because a woman who had suffered from a hemorrhage for twelve years and the dead daughter of a ruler seemed a bit remote). I wanted the congregation to think about themselves and about what it means to touch and to be touched. I think that the stories added contemporaneity to the sermon. But from the point of view of adding cognitive information, the stories did not need to be told. They dramatized, but did not move beyond the stated point.

Nonetheless, nonbiblical stories can be used in sermons for more than illustrative purposes. They, like the biblical stories themselves, can provide sermons with shape, movement, and content. I think that I learned this for the first time during my pulpit ministry in the 1960s. I also learned how powerful such stories can be in enabling recognition of one's self and one's time, and in opening up new possibilities for the future.

For a major part of the sixties, I served a parish in an eastern city threatened by racial violence. During a particularly violent week, I was asked by a group of the congregation's deacons to address specifically the question of race in my sermon for the following Sunday. I readily agreed to their request, but I had little idea of how to go about it. I had spoken on racial matters before; in fact, it was a rare sermon when the issue of race was nowhere present. I had pleaded often with the members of my all-white church for racial understanding, tolerance, and reconciliation. I am sure that I scolded them (and myself) on more than one occasion and exhorted them and got angry with them because a raging racism did not abate. By and large, those descendants of European immigrants stubbornly saw local blacks as intruders, foreign invaders who threatened their jobs, their homes, and their families. Frequent references were made to their laziness, their lack of education, and their low-grade values. Scolding did no good. Neither did quotations from the Commission on Civil Rights. Neither did the retelling of biblical texts with interpretive conclusions. How could I honor my deacons' request in a way that had any chance of changing attitudes and behavior?

I decided that I could not do better that next Sunday than by telling two human stories and by noting the similarities and the dissimilarities between them. I began by telling the story of my father who came to the United States as an eighteen-year-old boy. As I worked through the details of my dad's story, I began to realize that it was the story of most of the families in my parish: the unfading promise of a land of opportunity, combined with backbreaking hard work; adapting to a new environment while the language and customs of the homeland were no less highly honored; completed or advanced education while marriage was delayed; following where opportunity beckoned until the roots of job, family, and future were secure.

After telling my father's story (which was mine as well as theirs), I told the story of American blacks as best I could. They did not come to the United States because of an unfading promise. They were carried here and forced to work for the future of someone else. They were robbed of their former culture, given no chance to honor the customs and languages of their birthplace. They were denied education. They were kept rootless in a way in which nothing at all belonged to them—not their country, nor their past, not even their families. I asserted that their story is as real as that of my father. But it is quite a different story. And the differences help explain why things are the way they are. In order to understand, we must enter their story and stop trying to make them characters in ours. Such understanding is the only way to reconciliation.

I was surprised by the affirmative response to that sermon. Some said it was the most helpful that I had yet preached. Others said it enabled them to see all-too-familiar things in a new way. Still others thanked me for paying such tribute to my father and theirs while speaking words of reconciliation, which they knew they needed to hear. I say that I was surprised by such a positive response. And yet I have to admit that such a response was not totally unexpected. In using the two stories that I did, I felt that I had discovered what had been a missing element in my sermons. The narrative form that I had used regularly in retelling the story of the biblical text now began to give shape to what had been application by illustration or by direct address. ("The point of the biblical story has been made and it is clear. Now let me tell you the significance of that point for your lives.") In other words, my story, the story of my listeners, and our shared context were welcomed into my pulpit as a full partner in the preaching event. When the story of my congregants (at least the story of many of them) came alive in the sermon, I knew that they were not left to identify by analogy. Their identification, at least with my father, was immediate. I also knew that the stories I told gave them opportunity to focus where they wanted. The stories were not told in order to demonstrate a point. The stories *were* the point, and my listeners were given freedom to create their own meanings from the tales told. There was neither preface nor conclusion that told them what they must learn. Further, I knew that once my listeners had entered their story, they surrendered themselves to the logic and emotions of the narrative. They entered without knowing where they would be led. They willingly put themselves beyond guarantees, at the edge of their knowing. They put themselves at a place where they might be surprised by new learning and new possibilities.

For all my enthusiasm, however, I was also disturbed by my "people's narrative." I was certain that I had discovered the missing ingredient in my preaching. But I was afraid that in seizing it I had abandoned what was most essential. I cannot remember what the assigned biblical text was for the day that I preached the two stories. And I cannot remember whether I used it. If I did use it, it must have been as a reference point rather than as the hub from which all else came and to which all else returned. To make the biblical text peripheral, intentionally or not, conflicted with all of my training and with most of my practice of several years. What I said that day was not unbiblical. I am sure that it was informed by my understanding of the biblical material and witness. But I am also sure that what I said was biblical only in a general way. The specifics of no single text were present to expose or to enlighten. The details of no individual biblical story were present to complete or to challenge or to affirm the "people's narrative." Perhaps, I wondered, it is better after all to limit the nonbiblical story to illustration. I found myself worried about the fact that I may have discovered the nonbiblical story only to lose the Bible's. Such a trade might make for enthusiastic listening, but it would not necessarily provide for Christian proclamation. Such a trade might well mean the abandonment of my role as a teller of the tradition.

Needless to say, my frenzied concern was premature. I determined to relinquish neither the biblical narrative nor that of the people. Convinced that Christian preaching needs both, I began looking for the right combination or combinations. That search has now been carried out for a number of years. In a variety of settings I have persistently attempted to preach a combination of stories. I have experimented again and again, and have reflected seriously upon the occasions of those experiments. All in all, two things have made themselves clear. First, it is possible to maintain the centrality of both the biblical and nonbiblical stories. Second, there is no single model, no one right way to maintain such a dual centrality.

NARRATIVE OPTIONS

The Nonbiblical as Context

Several options are available to the preacher who wants to use both the biblical narrative and the narrative of the people. First, the nonbiblical story can be used to provide a context in which the biblical narrative can be heard with a sense of immediacy. A short while ago I preached a sermon on Gen. 50:15–21, the story of what happened between Joseph and his brothers upon the death of their father, Jacob. The story begins by focusing on the fear of the brothers: "It may be that Joseph will hate us and pay us back for all the evil which we did to him." In an attempt to give contemporary voice to the brothers' fear, I began the sermon by telling the story of Jake and Joey LaMotta (as narrated in the film, *Raging Bull*):

Jake and Joey LaMotta! Jake LaMotta, winner of eighty-three professional fights, and for two years middleweight champion of the world. And Joey—Jake's brother, friend, manager, confidant. Jake and Joey . . . of like-mind and like-spirit . . . inseparable . . . as close as two brothers can be. One day, for no real reason, Jake begins to suspect his wife Vicki of infidelity. Later, for even less reason, Jake begins to suspect that his brother Joey is the one with whom his wife has been unfaithful. Joey refuses to answer Jake's charges. "They're sick," he says, "and so are you." One afternoon, without warning, Jake bursts into his brother's apartment. He pushes the top half of Joey's body through a closed window. He beats Joey with his fists and knocks his own wife unconscious. Joey falls to the floor. Jake kicks his crumpled body. Then he leaves.

Many months later, Jake—no longer a champion or even a fighter, Jake, now an ex-con imprisoned on a morals charge, Jake, now an emcee in a sleazy strip joint, Jake—sees his brother Joey come out of a store. Jake calls, but Joey won't hear. Jake runs after his brother calling Joey's name, but Joey neither stops nor listens. Jake finally catches up to his brother as Joey is getting into his car. Clumsily, Jake puts his arms around his brother. "C'mon, Joey," he pleads. "That was a long time ago. Let's be friends." Jake kisses his brother's face, but Joey remains a voiceless statue. The embrace is not returned. The kisses are unanswered. Joey is deaf and lifeless. As Joey drives off, we hear Jake mutter, "Maybe you could call me sometime. . . ."

Joseph's brothers knew the sequence well. "It may be," they say, "that Joseph will hate us and pay us back for all the evil which we did to him." They knew the sequence well: transgression, hate, revenge. Life for life, eye for eye, tooth for tooth, hand for hand, foot for foot. That's the injunction. And we have not risen above it (the *lex talionis*). Such is the persistent story of our moral lives. Not only do we expect it, but we are encouraged to be disappointed when it doesn't occur.

Without forgetting the story of Jake and Joey, which is also our story, the sermon now centers on Joseph and his brothers, whose story is ours also. It narrates the counterstory that Joseph writes,

14

a story of forgiveness that does not excuse by overlooking the evil done. It narrates the fresh start and new beginning offered by this forgiveness. It tells of Joseph's remarkable insight into the larger story being written by God: "You meant evil against me; but God meant it for good. . . . So do not fear; I will provide for you and your little ones."

This option is probably the easiest to utilize. It is essential, of course, that the nonbiblical narrative echo that human drama that is explored by the biblical narrative. This can be problematic. A random human story is not sufficient. But while this option demands closely related biblical and nonbiblical stories, it keeps them relatively separate. The nonbiblical story serves as a prologue for the central biblical narrative. It can, as in the case of the sermon referred to here, give voice to only part of the biblical tale (the story of revenge rather than of forgiveness). Its function is to introduce, to provide a context for hearing as clearly as possible what the biblical text has to say to us.

The Nonbiblical as Conclusion

There is a second option for preachers who want to include both biblical and nonbiblical narrative in their sermons. This is more difficult to practice than the first. Here the nonbiblical story is used more as a demonstrative conclusion to the biblical story than as a prologue to the biblical tale. The biblical story is told and its natural conclusions allowed to surface. Then these conclusions are tested in the crucible of a nonbiblical story. If "tested" seems too strong a word, then "explored" can serve equally well. Here one of the distinctions between an illustration and a narrative becomes clearer. An illustration would be used to provide an example of the truth (i.e., claim, assertion) made. A narrative is used to test or to explore the same truth: Under what human circumstances is the claim true? Is it true for everyone? How does what is asserted actually play itself out in the daily lives of people like us? Needless to say, such a narrative must be accurate in its exploration. What is explored by the nonbiblical story must be that which has been asserted by the biblical one.

In a sermon on Matt. 11:25–30, I attempted to make use of this second option.[1] In telling the biblical narrative, I wrestled with the

15

meaning and the necessity of Jesus' words: "Come to me . . . take my yoke upon you . . . you will find rest . . . my yoke is easy and my burden is light." My retelling of the story led to the conclusion that Jesus was not speaking of rest as complete leisure or as total inactivity. He was talking about "refreshment, about zest for living, about a spring in the step that makes burdens lighter even as work goes on." But, I wondered, is this true? If one takes that claim out of the biblical story and puts it squarely in lives like ours, will it survive?

I explored and tested Jesus' words by telling the story of a phone conversation with a friend who lives many miles from me. My joy at hearing his voice soon faded as he told me about his crumbling life. Job, family, and health all seemed on the edge of ruin. He talked and I listened. After an hour or so, he let out a deep sigh. When I asked him what the sigh meant, he said, "I feel better now." I could not get over the seeming strangeness of his response. How could he feel better? His problems were still there. I had offered no sage advice or miracle restorer. Yet I knew that he meant what he said. And the truth was, I was feeling better myself. I concluded that Jesus' words were more true than I probably ever believed at any given moment. My friend felt better because he let go of his burden and gave part of it to me. But in giving it to me, he was really giving it to Jesus (acknowledged or not), the One who is "active in our conversations, planing yokes and easing wounds." I felt better because almost unintentionally I had been doing what I am supposed to do as a friend and as a Christian brother. I had taken Jesus' yoke upon myself. I had been called literally out of my own life into that of another.

A remarkable gift is given by use of this option. In this sermon, for example, I set out to explore the truth of Jesus' words. In doing so, I discovered meaning in Matt. 11:25–30 that I had not seen so clearly before. More than that, perhaps, I discovered something about my own life. My testing of the text ended in an explanation of my own life. While I explored the text, the text explored me. My conversation that night was not all that much. Certainly it was noted by the telephone company only as so many units of time. But the text informed me that in that conversation I had been wearing the yoke of Jesus. I had actually been participating in

Jesus' own work of giving rest. And the relief I felt soon turned to joy and gratitude.

Interweaving the Biblical and Nonbiblical

There is yet a third option for preachers who want to maintain the centrality of both biblical and nonbiblical narratives in their preaching. It is an option in which neither narrative serves as prologue or as explorative conclusion to the other. Here the biblical and nonbiblical narratives are interwoven in such a way that they form one story from beginning to end. While there is no single way in which this option may be fulfilled, it demands more skill than do the other options. This is so because the sermon that seeks to interweave the biblical and nonbiblical narratives must begin where many others end. That is to say, such a sermon begins only after the relation between the narratives has been explored. Such a sermon announces the relationship rather than explores it.

In a sermon preached on a recent Maundy Thursday, I attempted to announce the relationship between the assigned texts (Exod. 24:3–11, 1 Cor. 10:16–17, Mark 14:12–26) and a story about a certain Agnes Matson and myself. I did not use the full narrative of any of the biblical texts, but I did use their language and their claims. As much as anything, I wanted to connect four eucharistic meals: the one in Exodus 24, the one instituted by Jesus, the one we would be sharing that evening, and the one we would share in the "great and coming day." I also wanted to announce the significance of the Eucharist in a way that invited participation in it.

I told how Agnes, in her seventies, changed during the first two years of our relationship as pastor and parishioner. Suffering from senile dementia, she was transformed from a gentle woman, quick of mind and delicate of tongue, to a slow-witted and mean-tempered "crab" whom no one wanted to be around. Sometimes she would not even recognize me. Quite often she would refuse to see me. On some unforgettable days she would accuse me of stealing everything from her pet cat to the false teeth still in her mouth. Frequently I brought Agnes the sacramental meal and shared it with her. No matter how bizarre her initial behavior and no matter how awry her temperament, she always let me in. When

I gave her the bread, she always responded in the same way. "Oh, boy," she beamed, "does that taste good!"

I went on to say that Agnes continually made me aware that what I gave her was bread and that she and I together were human creatures who reaped where we did not sow and ate bread from a source far beyond ourselves. I admitted the frequent moments when I worried about Agnes's comprehension. Half the time she could not remember who she was. How could she understand Jesus' words about "my blood of the covenant"? How could she delight in the marvelous fulfillment of the eucharistic meal in Exodus 24: "They beheld God, and ate and drank"? I worried about her comprehension. And yet I knew that she did not have to be introduced to broken bread. She herself was broken. She herself existed as scraps torn from some wholeness: broken in body, crumbled in mind, split off from friendship, sliced away from all securities. Brokenness was the final question, not comprehension. I was as broken as she, bringing only scraps of fidelity, bits and pieces of love, crumbs of hope. When Agnes took the bread and exclaimed, "Oh boy, does that taste good," I think she was saying, "Brother Richard, both of us have tasted the kindness of the Lord."

I also admitted that it was not easy for me to visit Agnes. I never knew what to expect. But more than that, at each succeeding visit a lifetime of deep bitterness and rancor gushed out in a vitriolic flood. She cursed her condition, she denounced her sister, she damned people of other races, she indicted our congregation and my ministry. Often I became defensive and sometimes outright angry. And yet we were two broken people eating broken bread in which we were given to one another. I think that I learned in that nursing home why I need to eat Christ's meal often. I need to eat at this table of a family made one in Christ until the language, manners, memories, and tastes of that family become mine. I need to eat here until I am moved and softened to friendliness and service. Agnes has long been dead. I think of her frequently. She and I, along with all who share this meal, are still brothers and sisters. Each time we gather at this table we advance the great and coming day when Agnes, you and I, and the whole church, will feast with God in glory. Oh boy, Agnes, does that taste good!

NOTES

1. See "Weightlifting," in Richard L. Thulin, *The Caller and the Called* (Lima, Ohio: C.S.S. Publishing Co., 1986), 68–71.

Boy, Does That Taste Good!

Text: Exod. 24:3–11; 1 Cor. 10:16–17;
Mark 14:12–26

Agnes Matson was in her early seventies when I became her pastor. She was a demure, white-haired gentlewoman—quick of mind and delicate of tongue. To say that she was genteel would not be an overstatement. She was consistently elegant in manner and always free from rudeness. I visited Agnes and her sister frequently and always enjoyed my visits.

Two years after we met, Agnes had to be confined to a nursing home because of senile dementia. I continued to visit her over the next five years, but things were quite different. Her mind was no longer quick, nor her tongue delicate. Her consistency of manner swiftly deteriorated and I never knew what to expect. There were some few moments of lucidity, but on some days she did not even recognize me. On other days she recognized me but did not allow me to see her. On still other days, she recognized me, allowed me to see her, and then proceeded to accuse me of stealing everything from her pet cat to the false teeth still in her mouth.

Frequently I brought the sacrament to Agnes and shared that meal with her. No matter how bizarre her initial behavior, no matter how awry her temperament, she always let me in. And when I gave her the bread, a now inconsistent Agnes offered a repeatedly consistent response (yet one she never would have made in the years of her secure gentility). "Oh boy," she beamed, "does that taste good!" Oh boy, does that taste good!

Agnes always made me aware that what I gave her was bread: good-tasting, sweet-smelling, hunger-satisfying bread. She also made me aware that she and I together were human creatures, creatures of flesh and blood. We were human beings whose stomachs growled, whose saliva flowed, and whose taste buds danced in expectation and satisfaction. We were creatures who eat and drink, walk and sleep, talk and love, reaping where we did not sow and eating bread from a source far beyond ourselves.

I wonder if you have ever thought about the fact that you cannot adequately describe a scrap of bread without attempting to describe the whole universe? Even a scrap is a wonder. It is a transformation of rain and sunshine. It is a bit of matter, the name given for movement and space mysteriously confined within a definite shape. A bit of bread is possible not only because of the work of many hands, but because of a number of universal movements. Every time we eat bread we remember that we are creatures and we remember that our very existence depends upon the ceaseless work of God. Agnes and I together, two creatures taking bread and giving thanks: "Blessed art thou, Lord God, King of the Universe, who bringest forth bread from the earth."

There were times when I worried about Agnes's comprehension, about her discernment. Half the time she could not remember her own name or where she was. How could she understand Jesus' words about "my blood of the covenant"? How could she delight in the marvelous fulfillment in our midst of that eucharistic meal in Exodus 24: "They beheld God, and ate and drank"? Things like that worried me. I do not finally know what Agnes comprehended. But I do know that she did not need to be introduced to broken bread. When I handed her the scrap of bread, I imagined that she felt as if she were looking in a mirror. She herself was broken. She herself existed as scraps torn from some wholeness: broken in body, crumbled in mind, split off from friendships, sliced away from securities. I knew her brokenness. At those moments I was not as concerned about her comprehension as about her brokenness—about her brokenness and my own. When I sat with her, I was not broken in body or mind (although there is always some of that in each of us), but I had, as always, only scraps of fidelity, bits and pieces of love and crumbs of love. There we sat, two people so different in many ways, yet two broken people clutching broken bread.

"This is the body of Christ given (broken) for you," I said to both of us. And when Agnes said, "Oh boy, does that taste good," she may have been saying far more than she or I thought. Just maybe she was saying, "Brother Richard, we have tasted the kindness of the Lord. Brother Richard, we have tasted the Lord and seen that the Lord is good." It has never seemed strange to me that at the breaking of the bread, at the fracturing and splitting of the bread, we are usually silent. The reality of what happens is beyond our power to express. The body of our Lord once given *for* us is now given *to* us. The body of our Lord, broken in order to be shared, is given for our brokenness. It is given so that our broken lives may be restored as members of his body.

It was not always easy for me to visit Agnes. Clock time meant nothing. A call ahead did not mean that she would be ready for a visit. I could never anticipate her mood. It was almost impossible to carry on any kind of a normal conversation. Worst of all, I guess, was the fact that deep bitterness and rancor, seemingly held in check by her gentility, came gushing out in a vitriolic flood. She cursed her condition. She denounced her sister. She scolded the nurses and other guests. She disparaged some races and damned others. She indicted our congregation and my ministry. It was difficult for me to listen to such hostility. Even making allowances for her condition, I was often defensive and sometimes outright angry. And yet, there we were, two broken people with broken bread in which we were given to one another. Bread was broken so that our acquaintanceship could become friendship. We who formerly meant nothing to each other were now brother and sister in Christ. "Take, this is my body. Because there is one loaf, we who are many are one body." We *are* the body as we feed upon the body. We are limbs of Christ's flesh and bone.

As I struggled with our oneness and our ofttimes vehemence toward each other, I found Luther helpful. If you want to be sure you have profitably partaken of the Lord's Supper, Luther said, observe your conduct toward your neighbor. Do not reflect on the great devoutness you experienced. Do not reflect on the sweetness of the words in your head. You will know that the sacrament is efficacious, Luther said, when you are moved and softened to be friendly to your enemy, to take an interest in your neighbor's welfare, to help your neighbor bear suffering and affliction. Without this there is not certainty of the sacrament's effectiveness even if you communed seven hundred times a day with devotions so great as to move you to tears.

Perhaps in that nursing home I learned a firm reason for my frequent communion. I need to eat at this table of a family made one in Christ. I need to eat here until the language of that family, the manners and memories and tastes of that family, become mine. I need to eat here until I am moved and softened to friendliness and interest and service. And maybe that is why Agnes and I ate so many communion meals together.

Agnes Matson has long been dead. I think of her often. She and all with whom you and I share this meal are still brothers and sisters. Each time we gather at this table, we advance by anticipation the great and coming day, the day when Agnes, you, I, and the whole church, gathered into God's Kingdom, will feast with God in glory. Oh boy, Agnes, does that taste good!

Amen. Come, Lord Jesus.

TWO

The Parameters of Narrative Preaching

LUCY ROSE

Christina collected her books in a hurry and left the classroom. "That professor's an idiot!" she muttered to herself. "An idiot! All sermons *don't* have to have three points."

Never glancing up, she brushed past several people on the steps to the first floor. Outside, the sunshine filtered through tall shade trees along the walkway to her dorm. Her seminary experience so far had been hard, especially courses in church history. But *preaching!* she thought. Maybe I ought to quit and go back to teaching high school. She chuckled at her escapist attitude and sighed, Why am I so mad about that lecture? I want to be a good preacher. I really want to learn what Dr. Smithy has to teach me. She managed to smile at friends Jay and Gail. Her room offered a welcome retreat. She threw the books on her desk and sprawled on the bed.

"I can't preach three-point sermons. *I won't.* But what's the alternative? Dr. Smithy sure did put down narrative sermons. What'd he call them? 'Preacherly storytelling.' I wonder what narrative preaching really is. I'm glad I have six weeks before I have to preach in class." She was talking to herself again, sometimes silently, sometimes out loud, sorting out the conflicts, reclaiming her convictions. She looked at the clock—11:30. The cafeteria would open in an hour for lunch. Maybe in the meantime she could begin to make some sense out of the chaos inside.

Images crowded, pushing and shoving into her consciousness. She focused on one: Her father is preaching. Tears run down her face as he tells of when their dog Spots was killed by a car. His point is etched in her memory—like her sister bending over the limp dog, sobbing "Spottie, please, don't die." So God cries over the world, "Souls of men, why will you die? God, your Maker, asks you why." She thought to herself, That's from somewhere in Ezekiel. And I'd change the male language, but that's the way Daddy used to say it. Her father . . . sermons . . . Spots . . . stories.

Another image claimed her attention: She is a child and it's bedtime. Her mother is reading to her. She wondered what the book was—*The Wizard of Oz* or another of the Oz series about Dorothy? Frances Hodgson Burnett's *The Secret Garden* or *The Little Princess*? Maybe *Alice in Wonderland*. No, she thought. I read that one to myself. Why have those particular titles come to my mind? She lay still, waiting for the answer to swim up from the depths inside. With a laugh she said out loud, "They're all about girls, about freethinking Dorothys caught up in an unusual adventure. Like me here at seminary. No languishing beauty asleep till the Prince arrives. No Rapunzel waiting to be rescued. In the stories I remember Mama reading to me, the main characters were active and independent. Was it Bettelheim who claimed that stories shape children's lives? As we identify with the characters, we are actually changed by their adventures."[1]

Christina felt a thrill of insight. "That's the spectrum. My father's sermons on one side as point sermons at their best. And Dorothy and the Wizard of Oz on the other side as a story that has radically influenced my life."

Again she lay still, thinking for a long time. Then she picked up a pen and a piece of paper and charted her thoughts:

Point sermons	*Stories*
stories illustrate truth	stories are truth in themselves
deductive	inductive
Jung's category: thinking	Jung's category: feeling

She knew the two ends of the spectrum overlapped. There was

more thinking to be done. But now it was time for lunch. Maybe, she thought, I'll run into that new guy, Brad. He's cute. Where'd he transfer from?

After lunch Christina stopped by the bookstore and bought a spiral notebook. Back in her room she found a wide-tipped, blue magic marker and wrote on the cover, "The Case Against Dr. Smithy: What Is Narrative Preaching?" Inside she recopied her jottings from the morning. Satisfied that she had made a valiant beginning, she put the notebook aside and turned to her assigned theology reading.

Christina's next entry in her notebook started like this. (See Figure 1.)

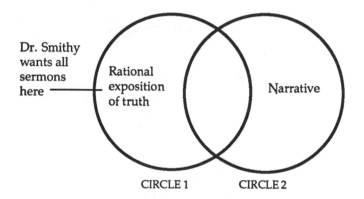

Circle 1: sermons as rational exposition of truth
Circle 2: the broad homiletical category called "narrative"

Figure 1

Her entry continued, "Many sermons fall outside the middle ground because they are unaffected by the adjacent area. For example, in the left part of Circle 1, the part that doesn't overlap, would be the sermon I heard last Sunday at Shadybrook. It was like a lecture—three points, no illustrations, not even a poem, just a deductive explanation of 'what it means to be justified.' Boring! It made faith so unrelated to life. I wonder if Dr. Smithy would have liked it. The sermon I read by Paul Tillich and the one by Reinhold Niebuhr belong in the left part of circle 1 also. They were interesting and full of challenging ideas, but had no narrative content.

"I need to read more about Circle 2. Note to myself: Get Eugene Lowry's *The Homiletical Plot* and *Doing Time in the Pulpit*. Check on other resources.

"P.S. Talked to Brad after church Sunday at Shadybrook."

Christina never opened her polity book that evening. Instead, she worked on her "Case against Dr. Smithy" notebook, redrawing the circles she'd drawn several weeks earlier. (See Figure 2.)

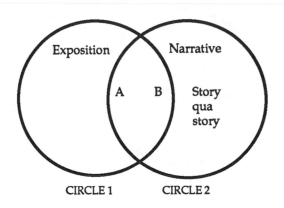

Figure 2

Then she wrote, "What is Circle 2, the narrative circle, all about? I think it has three sections: (1) story qua story to the far right where there's almost no influence from Circle 1; (2) area A, left perimeter of the middle; and (3) area B, the right perimeter of the middle. My father's sermons are near A: feelings and illustrations always support analysis. He'll start with a point and then use illustrations—sometimes very emotion-charged stories—to clarify, to relate to real life, and/or to drive home the truth he's focusing on. His sermons might look like this." (See Figure 3.)

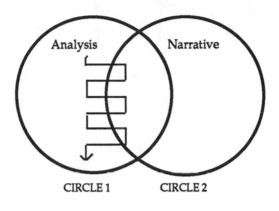

CIRCLE 1   CIRCLE 2

Figure 3

"There's movement in and out of the two fields.
"But rational logic controls the movement.
"Smithy would like these sermons."

Christina put down her pen and thought of the Sunday in her summer field-assignment church when she'd preached on the story of Naaman from 2 Kings 5:1–19. She'd basically told the biblical story and stopped three times to draw lessons from the narrative. Then she remembered her sermon for Youth Sunday at her home church, on the experience of Rhoda in Acts 12:12–17. She'd introduced Rhoda as a guest speaker at the beginning and at the end made the point that "there is joy in the heart of every believer who comes face to face with the risen Christ." Now she wrote, "I might diagram my Naaman sermon like this." (See Figure 4.) "I started in the story but came out to make three deductive points."

"My Rhoda sermon might look like this." (See Figure 5.) "The bulk of the sermon was a retelling of the story, but the 'point' was presented explicitly, almost extrinsically to the story.

27

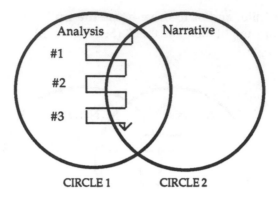

Figure 4

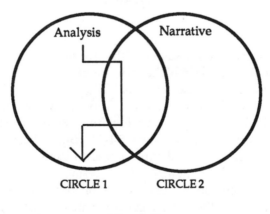

Figure 5

"Tentative conclusion: My father's sermons are not narrative; my Naaman and Rhoda sermons were. Why? I think because in most of my father's sermons the movement of thought is controlled by analytical thought; in my Naaman and Rhoda sermons the movement of thought is controlled by the biblical story. In the former, feelings and illustrations support and give insight to rational thought; in the latter, rational thought supports and gives insight to the biblical story.

"For those sermons that fall in area A on the diagram, Eugene Lowry has been most helpful. Lowry talks about the sermon's movement being like a story's plot—a move from disequilibrium to equilibrium, from conflict to resolution. Sarah Johnston's sermon in chapel was like this. (The one Dr. Smithy hated and said so in class on Tuesday.) She set up the tension in the Good Samaritan story. Then she posited the priest and Levite as a resolution that doesn't work, that is, we can't walk by forever. Then she presented the 'correct' resolution—stopping and helping—that led to more tension, that is, we can't and don't want to stop and help the communist, the street person, the AIDS victim, with that kind of selfless abandon. More tension. But the 'go and do likewise' is possible *by God's grace*. True resolution. Rev. Johnston used Clarence Jordan's *Cottonpatch Gospel* as a conclusion—as we've experienced rejection and grace, so we can offer grace to another who is rejected. Her plot[2] unfolded this way:

conflict → false resolution → continuing conflict →
resolution → new conflict → true resolution

"Wow! That's a lot like that Chekhov short story, 'Grief,'[3] in which the emotions of a cab driver, unable to talk about his son's death because no one will listen, carry the plot along. It moves from conflict to no resolution several times. Each time the conflict builds, until the resolution comes at the end.

"Maybe I'll try a sermon like that. I could use the passage I've been working on, the woman with the flow of blood in Mark 5:24–34. The introduction will draw us, the hearers and me, into the story as those in search of wholeness.

"First we'll stand in the shoes of the crowd. We're spectators to the healing, and we leave the story untouched by Jesus' grace. No resolution.

"Then we'll stand in the shoes of Jesus, a point of view Christians often take when reading Scripture. But again we leave the story unchanged. No resolution.

"Then we'll stand in the shoes of the disciples. They even have a speaking part. But their role is far from noble. In their practicality they almost miss the miracle that brings wholeness. No resolution.

"Last we'll stand in the shoes of the woman. We'll have to admit our uncleanness not only to ourselves but to Jesus and to the crowd; 'she told the whole truth' (v. 33). Then Jesus sends her/us off in peace. Her healing is more than just physical; she experiences Jesus' gift of wholeness. And maybe we can, too.

"Funny, the plot of both this sermon and the Chekhov story is like one Smithy put on the board the other day:

1. Not this
2. Not this
3. Not this
4. But this

"The same plot can be in Circle 1 or Circle 2. What makes the difference? I think the sermon I'm describing would be narrative because the movement is controlled not by objective logic, not even by the biblical story—because I'd retell it four times—but by the logic of the heart searching for wholeness. I think that's what Lowry means by a plot. This sermon would go on the right end of the middle, the B area. Again, Dr. Smithy wants rational logic to control the movement of sermons. I wonder what Smithy would think if I preached this 'woman with the flow of blood' sermon in class."

Christina closed the notebook. There was still time to read at least a part of the polity assignment. She could read the rest in the morning.

Christina's next entry in the notebook went like this: "Reading and collecting more evidence in my case against Dr. Smithy. What is narrative preaching? Read *Preaching Biblically*, edited by Don M. Wardlaw. Brad recommended it. It has some good examples of narrative preaching. They confirm my categories from last entry. Several are narrative because the basic plot of the sermon follows the biblical story, with thoughtful reflection subordinated to the story. Others are narrative because the plot, as in short stories, moves from conflict to resolution. At least one is close to story qua story. At least one is not narrative because the movement is controlled by objective logic.

"If the movement of thought is the key element, would the term *deductive* apply to non-narrative sermons, and *inductive* to narrative? Or what's so special about narrative-sermon movement that doesn't just follow the biblical story?

"I hope I can figure out this narrative preaching stuff soon—I preach in two weeks!"

Christina turned off the alarm after four hours of sleep. She thought, Funny how your mind works while you're asleep. I'm probably going to fail polity, exegesis, and theology. And if I preach my "woman with the flow of blood" sermon next week, I'll fail preaching. But I think I've solved the last riddle.

Inductive Preaching by Lewis and Lewis lay beside her pillow. It had kept her up till 3:30 A.M. She placed it on top of Craddock's *As One Without Authority*. Seeing her "Case Against Dr. Smithy" notebook, she announced to nobody in particular, "I'm going to make *one more entry* and close this case for good." Tripping on the rug between the bed and the bathroom, she added, "I hope I make it through this day. I think I'm crazy. Somebody should give me credit for all this extra work I'm doing."

Brad was leaving his room at the same time as Christina was heading to breakfast.

"Listen, Brad. You've got to eat breakfast with me and listen to my most recent discovery."

"Fine," Brad mumbled. He was still trying to wake up, but Christina's excitement made him smile. "I'm not usually worth much before 10:00 in the morning, but I'll do my best. As my dad used to say, 'Start talking.' "

"Well, you see, the word *inductive* has bothered me since I began this narrative preaching project. Is all narrative preaching inductive? My supervising pastor last summer suggested I read Craddock's *As One Without Authority*. So I did. Have you read it?"

Brad shook his head. "Should have," he muttered to himself.

"No problem—it talks about the need for inductive preaching, preaching that doesn't have all the answers. For Craddock, deductive, didactic, Smithy-type sermons are out. Out!"

"So—" she paused. "You know my categories, don't you?"

Brad nodded.

"I started with *inductive* as a word that belongs on the narrative side. But I wanted to pursue the meaning of the word further. So last night I read a book called *Inductive Preaching*. I thought it'd have all the answers, but I was wrong. I stayed up till 3:29 reading and thinking. But this morning everything is clear. Are you taking all this in?"

"Uh huh." Brad smiled a more awake smile.

They had reached the dining hall by now, got their trays and selected a table in the corner away from most of the other students. Christina did not wait to put her tray down before she was talking again.

"This morning it was all clear. But it'll take a while for me to explain it. Okay?"

"I said it was okay. I'll *eat* and *listen* at the same time."

"Oh, sure," said Christina. "You see Lewis and Lewis, a father-son team, define *inductive* simply as inverted deductive. Do you have a pencil?"

Brad had a pen in his shirt pocket. She grabbed it, jotted down an outline on her napkin, and explained, "Deductive looks like this:

I
A
II
A
B

"Now the way Lewis and Lewis define *inductive*, it looks like this:

A
I
A
B
II

"The A's and B's are the particulars: the illustrations, examples, or statistics. In deductive thinking they *prove* the point that has already been made. But they *lead to* the point in the Lewis and Lewis inductive method. And that is *one* definition of the word.

"I think what came to me in my sleep was an experience I had last summer. I was driving home from church and I stopped at a stop sign. A woman approached from the left in her car, slowed up, and stopped; but she didn't have a stop sign. She just stopped. I was really upset. Should I go ahead because she was being an idiot? Should I wait for her to realize she didn't have a stop sign? That could be an hour! After a few moments I started to go. She started to go. I slammed on the brakes and motioned angrily to her to go on. Then I went on. On the way home I formulated a conclusion—that someone who doesn't know the rules of the road is as dangerous as someone who breaks the law. That's inductive thinking—Lewis and Lewis style—moving from the particular, the experience, to the general, the principle. Do you follow?"

"Yeah, it's interesting," Brad replied, looking more awake.

"I was staying with a Mrs. Dowinger then, and when I got home, I announced my conclusion to her. She was at the kitchen table shelling peas when I began by saying, 'Do you know that people who don't know the law can be as dangerous as those who break the law?' 'Huh?' she said. 'Run that by me again.' I repeated my truth triumphantly, expecting her to grasp its profundity. She shook her head, 'I guess what you're saying is true, Christina. But I'm really not sure what you mean.' So I had to tell her about my experience to prove, to illustrate, to make sense of my principle. That's deductive." Christina pointed to the design on the napkin:

I

A

"Conclusion followed by supportive evidence." She looked at Brad.

"Okay, I understand," Brad said, pointing to the outlines on the napkin. "That's deductive and that's inductive."

"No!" Christina almost shouted. "My whole point is that's not the *only* definition of *inductive*. May I borrow your napkin?" Not waiting for an answer, she reached for it and drew her familiar circles, placing an asterisk in the left of Circle 1.

"Lewis and Lewis go here," she announced, pointing to the asterisk. "They're *not* narrative. They use stories to prove points but their real interest is in ideas, points, truths—just like Dr. Smithy.

"Now Craddock is a different story. He uses a totally different definition of *inductive*. But it's a valid definition. While I was asleep I must have remembered an experience I had in an education course at college. The class started with a movie.[4] The first thing you see is a hand filling a glass from a pitcher. So there are two clear glasses full of clear liquid on the table. The hand puts an ice cube in one glass, pushes it to the bottom with a spoon, and it pops back up. The hand puts an ice cube in the second glass, pushes it to the bottom with the spoon and it rises only about an inch. It stays near the bottom of the glass. Slowly it rises to about the middle. The hand pushes the cube in the first glass down and again it pops back to the top. When the cube in the second glass is pushed down, it rises slowly to the middle, then gradually climbs closer to the top. A third time the ice is pushed down. This time both cubes rise to the top.

The movie ended and the professor told us she would answer yes-or-no questions until we figured out why the ice cubes had acted differently. It was fun. I was the one who asked if there was a difference in the temperature of the water. The professor said yes. It turned out the second glass was warmer than room temperature and contained a mixture of alcohol and water. After the questioning time, we reflected on the process of asking questions. Which questions had been helpful? Why? Which questions had been wasted, so to speak? Why? The important thing wasn't the answer to the puzzle but the process, the learning to think, the experience of asking questions and reflecting on asking questions. In this case the word *inductive* means a process that helps people learn to think. Now that's exactly what Craddock means by *inductive* in his book. Here, I wrote down a quote." She read from a folded piece of notebook paper that she had fished from her pocket. It said:

The sole purpose [of preaching] is to engage the hearer in the pursuit of an issue or an idea so that he [or she] will think his [or her] own thoughts and experience his [or her] own feelings in the presence of Christ and in the light of the Gospel.[5]

"Craddock even says the sermon shouldn't be a package tied up with a bow by the end. Rather the hearer participates in the sermon and finishes it in whatever way fits his or her own life. Completing the thought, the movement, the decision-making is the task of the hearer, not the preacher. See! It's the *process* that's important. The goal isn't rational truth at all but participation in an experience that's open-ended. Craddock's definition of *inductive* definitely fits under the heading 'narrative preaching.' There's an edge of narrative preaching here, . . ." she said as she labeled the left side of circle 1 with an A, "that's not Craddockly inductive." Having coined this adverb, she raised her eyebrows at Brad and grinned. "Those sermons often just follow the biblical story and make points related to life. But Craddock's kind of inductive spans the rest of the narrative circle. I wonder what it feels like to preach that kind of a sermon?" She paused. "Anyway, there you have it. Case closed. All that's left is to write all I've been saying to you in my notebook."

Brad said, teasingly, "And to preach your sermon in class next Tuesday."

"Don't remind me!"

"Hey, come on. We're gonna be late to class."

"This sermon just won't come together!" Christina complained. "And I've got to preach it tomorrow." It was Saturday morning. She had finished the exegesis; she was using the same passage she had chosen for her exegesis paper and had been brainstorming off and on for a week. This was a dry run for Dr. Smithy's sermon Tuesday. She'd focused on a single message. But there was no form, no shape, no points, no thought-blocks, no moves. Nothing.

Maybe her message wasn't precise enough. Christina mentally reviewed her material. The text was the words of Jesus, "This is my blood . . . poured out for many" (Mark 14:24). Her focus was on the words as both a description of life and an invitation to live as Jesus lived—poured out for many. Either way they are frighten-

35

ing words. To give ourselves to others, to be poured out for others, is frightening. She'd thought about both the Lowry books and had identified the conflict, the tension, the starting point.

Her normal sermon design was what she called a *collage*—a linear sequence of blocks. But right now no sequence would emerge. In fact no clear blocks of thought were evident. Nothing was right this time.

She put down her pencil and legal pad and stared at the books, some open, some closed, on the bed around her. She glanced at the desktop to her left. A stack of file folders lay within reach. Absent-mindedly she picked up the one on top. In it were odd things she had written for a course in religion and the arts in college. She began reading a fairy tale she had written as a course project. The story was better than she remembered. At the end the professor had written, "A good story. It has great potential. Tighten the language. My thirteen-year-old loved it!" She lingered over a few more items in the folder—beginnings of two other fairy tales, several poems, and reminiscences.

Automatically she retrieved the pencil and the legal pad. She began: "Louisa sat in a hard, metal chair and tried to listen to the sermon. Her church was different from most. . . ."

Several hours later she put the pencil down again. On the paper was half of a story—pure story—without third-person reflections and didactic asides. There was only a young girl's mental struggle to understand the meaning of communion and especially the symbol of "blood . . . poured out for many."

"I don't know if I'll preach this or not," Christina said out loud. "I'd better test it out."

It wasn't like any sermon she'd ever written before. Here was story qua story.

Christina's insides were turning somersaults as she knocked on Brad's door.

"Oh, Christina, come in."

Christina's voice was tentative, almost trembling, "Could you do me a favor?"

"Sure!"

"Would you listen to something I wrote? I'm not sure it's a

sermon, but I might preach it tomorrow down at the church I served last summer. It's different. Dr. Smithy wouldn't approve *at all*."

"Well, let's hear it."

Christina read in a flat, uninvolved voice. This wasn't Louisa's story. It was her own. She was vaguely afraid of it. A central image was of Louisa thinking of herself as a pitcher. During the day the water in the pitcher was used up, poured out for others, till only a few drops were left. Christina got to the bottom of page five; Louisa was babysitting. Christina read, "How do you keep going when the pitcher's empty? How do you keep from throwing two smelly, uncaring babies right out the bathroom window? When there's nothing left to give, how can you keep on giving of your time, of your energy, of your self?"

Each word caught in her throat. She forced herself to keep reading, "Yes, she *was* a pitcher of water poured out—no, she was a pitcher of blood poured out, only when the blood was gone, she wasn't dead. She had to go on breathing, changing dirty diapers, gently putting two spiteful kids back in the playpen. Two tears wet the corners of her eyes. She looked up."

Christina looked up from the manuscript. Tears pressed against the edges of her eyes. "Sorry, Brad. I didn't realize how much of me was in this." She sighed a deep sigh and went on, ending with the words on page eight, which reflected Louisa's thoughts, "But even if that's true—that God refills our pitchers—that's not enough. I mean that's what I've heard all my life. God gives to us; we give to others. We give and give and give till the pitcher's empty and then some. Well, that isn't fair! I can't give what's not there! The God pitcher doesn't come around often enough. Yet people always seem to want more—especially Sara Louise. Something's missing."

After a pause Christina said, "Well, that's as far as I've gotten. What do you think? Can I preach it?"

"It's wonderful." Brad's face was pensive. Then he smiled a big, open, reassuring smile. "Of course you can preach it. I want to know how it ends."

"Thanks." That was exactly what she needed to hear. She had given speech to the disequilibrium. She wasn't quite sure how it would end, but the resolution was inside her. She'd wait. It would come.

"By the way, Christina, how does this fit into the case against Dr. Smithy?"

Christina shook her head, "I don't know. I had thought the case was closed. But I think writing this sermon is a really important step. I'll know more tomorrow. Thanks for listening. I might even preach this one for Dr. Smithy. What do you think he'd say?"

"He'd die. Then he'd fail you."

"Oh, well. I still have three days. Thanks again."

"How'd the sermon go this morning?" Brad asked as he set his tray down on the cafeteria table across from Christina. "I've thought about you off and on all day."

"It went fine."

"What'd people say?" Brad prodded.

"A lot of people said that it really spoke to them. Several folks just hugged me real tight. One woman thanked me for . . ."— Christina spoke slowly, trying to remember the right words— "allowing . . . a place . . . for fantasy. She said so many sermons and so much of worship are just consciousness. I think that's the word she used. Consciousness, thinking, rational stuff. I think she said her name was Dede. She wasn't there last summer."

Brad interjected, "Sounds like your sermon was a real hit."

"Yeah, I guess. Let me tell you about this other woman, okay?"

"Sure."

"She said—and I remember this word for word—'I'm not sure I understood the sermon but it made me teary. It made me want to cry.' What do you make of that? What do you think she meant?"

Brad began to play with his soup spoon. "Seems to me she's expressing both a strength and a danger of preaching just pure story. Faith is certainly deeper than what we can verbalize. I think it's important to have experiences of faith that aren't analytical, or rational, to use your word. What'd Paul say in Romans about 'sighs too deep for words'? Well, maybe your sermon touched her where there are feelings too deep for words. And I think that's important."

"So what's the danger?" Christina asked.

"Well, if all sermons were stories, our faith wouldn't be very reflective. A congregation would have faith *experiences* week after week, but they'd never learn how to *think* about them, how to reflect theologically on what they've experienced. It seems like over the long haul a congregation needs both story to evoke experience and rational thought to bring to consciousness the meaning of the experience." He fell silent.

Christina swallowed the last bite of her cheese sandwich, and responded, "That makes a lot of sense. And what Dr. Smithy denies is the power of narrative to produce experience. But if you're right, then he's right in that there's a need for—what'll I call it—theological analysis. He just wants analysis all the time. You know, I'm not as angry at him as I was. But there's still no way I'm going to preach a three-point sermon on Tuesday. Did you go to Shadybrook this morning?"

Brad nodded, "And Dr. Turner lectured again. If my aunt and uncle didn't go there and take me home with them for Sunday dinner, I'd go somewhere else. But it's the only home cooking I get these days. By the way, thanks for going with me the other Sunday. We'd better go read theology or we'll be in trouble tomorrow. Or have you read it?"

"Naw. Let's go."

"Christina, will you preach the Louisa sermon in class on Tuesday?"

Christina shut her eyes and whispered, "I don't know."

It was Monday night. The light was on in Christina's room when Brad returned to the dorm from the library. He knocked.

"How's it coming?" he asked when she opened the door.

"Oh, Brad. I'm a coward. I've spent all semester figuring out what narrative preaching is just to prepare my case against Dr. Smithy. I've even mentally written the screenplay for what's going to happen tomorrow. I'd preach my Louisa sermon. I'd be so confident that I'd be able to look at Dr. Smithy turning redder and redder as his anger escalated. Then I'd look at you and Gail and Jay and you'd all be smiling and nodding and laughing inside at how I was putting one over on Dr. Smithy. Then in the evaluation session Dr. Smithy'd fire at me first with both barrels of the shotgun and then with the cannons. He'd be so mad. And I'd just wait. After his tirade he'd just sit there smoldering, ready for the discussion, as he calls it. Then I'd begin my rebuttal. I've learned all kinds of support from lots of homileticians. I can *prove* he's outdated to insist that all sermons be rational and analytical. It'd be a grand moment." She wrinkled her nose. "Granted I'd probably get an F on the sermon, but I think I could pull a C out of the course with the other work I've done and the exam. It'd be worth it."

"Then what do you mean, you're a coward?"

"I got scared. I copped out. I have written the most wonderful three-point sermon you'll ever hear."

Brad smiled a wry smile and shook his head.

"Seriously, Brad. It isn't bad. I even have a tear-jerker story near the end. But I might not be able to use it; it makes me cry to tell it. It sounds like a sermon my father might preach. And learning how to preach Dr. Smithy's way has merits—a congregation needs theological reflection. Even you said so." She sighed. "I'm ashamed of myself."

"Are you really?" Brad picked up the "Case Against Dr. Smithy" notebook. "You're not one for confrontation. But you are one to finish a task you've set for yourself." He chucked the notebook back on the desk. "That's the finished product. That notebook is the magnum opus of your seminary career." Now his smile was open and affirming. "Preach your three-point sermon. Get your A. And one day when you take Dr. Smithy's place, *you'll* teach preaching differently."

POSTSCRIPT

I wrote the Louisa sermon shortly before starting this chapter. Writing that sermon was a breakthrough in my understanding of the spectrum of narrative preaching, especially of such terms as *plot* and *inductive*. I was fascinated by, but not adept at, the "Craddockly" inductive approach of drawing people into a process of thinking their own thoughts. I knew there was a lot of rational thought related to what I wanted to say in this chapter, and I was afraid those sections would be boring as straight analysis. It occurred to me to shape a story that would say all that I wanted to say via an imaginative, inductive plot, and so I chose this format for telling the essential data of my own journey toward narrative preaching. This chapter represents the culmination of my thoughts about how I define the spectrum called *narrative preaching*.

NOTES

1. Bruno Bettelheim, *The Uses of Enchantment* (New York: Vintage Books, 1977).

2. I am indebted to Tom Long and Ron Allen for their sermons in *Preaching Biblically*, ed. Don M. Wardlaw (Philadelphia: Westminster Press, 1983), which inspired this sermon "plot."

3. "Grief," in *The Stories of Anton Chekhov*, ed. Robert N. Unscott (New York: Modern Library, 1932), 103–9.

4. J. Richard Suchman, *Inquiry Development Program in Physical Science: Teacher's Guide* (Chicago: Science Research Associates, Inc., 1966), 47–48.

5. Fred B. Craddock, *As One Without Authority: Essays on Inductive Preaching* (Enid, Okla.: Phillips University Press, 1971), 157.

Body Broken, Blood Spilled

Text: 2 Sam. 23:13–17; Mark 14:22–24

Louisa sat in a hard metal chair and tried to listen to the sermon. Her church was different from most. Last month she'd gone to church with her best friend Susan and sat in pews, looking at rows and rows of backs of heads. She liked her church better—two rows of chairs in a horseshoe. She could see faces and watch expressions. She knew certain faces were open with simple emotions; others kept secrets. Sometimes when everyone else laughed, Mr. Henderson seemed to frown and his eyes dropped to study his fidgety hands. And Mrs. Wisecoff . . .

"Here I am again," Louisa chided herself. "Daydreaming! What is the preacher saying?" She wished she could pay more attention.

The communion table was empty today. Last week there had been a pitcher of wine, two chalices, two plates, and a loaf of bread. The bread was always tasty with chewy seeds her mama never used in cooking. She didn't like the taste of wine much, but she never drank much, just enough to wet the tip of her tongue. What did it all mean, the communion, the Lord's Supper? It was something they did once a month. She knew all the proper theological words to describe what they were doing. But what did it mean *to her*, to *Louisa*, on *this* day, June 14, 1987?

> The bread, the body of Christ, broken,
> the wine, Jesus' blood, poured out.

She knew what each word meant: bread/wine, body/blood, broken/poured. Broken . . . poured out.

She thought of the pitcher of water she had dropped the day before. Her Saturday chore was to water the philodendron, the Norfolk Island pine, and the Christmas cactus her mother tried to keep alive from month to month. They were surviving better now that Louisa was giving them regular care. Yesterday she'd tripped on the rug in the hall. She hadn't hurt herself, but the pitcher had broken into a hundred pieces and the water had spilled all over the rug. Mama had helped her clean up the mess.

> body broken, like that pitcher
> blood poured out, like water on the rug
>   soaked up . . . gone . . . no way to get it back
> Jesus' body broken, Jesus' blood poured out
>   no way to put Humpty Dumpty together again. She wondered if
> that last thought was sacrilegious.

Then the words of her Sunday school teacher that morning echoed in her ears. Mrs. Otis had said, "Christians are to be like Jesus. Always ask yourself, 'What would Jesus do?' " Louisa could almost get the right tone of voice. She grinned to herself. She liked Mrs. Otis, but she was real old-fashioned. Be like Jesus. . . .

> Be like Jesus
> Be like that pitcher
>   the handle by the bedroom door,
>   the base beside the bookcase,
>   odd-sized pieces scattered between
>   and the water only a big spot on the rug

She tried to think of herself as that pitcher. It sort of made her scared. . . .

> being broken up
> her insides a spot on the rug
> like a car accident she'd seen in a movie one time.

No! She didn't want her body broken or her blood spilled out.

If that's what communion meant, she didn't want to be like Jesus. Water poured out, a pitcher of water. . . . Maybe, maybe she *was* like a pitcher of water.

Like last Friday! She'd bounded out of bed, much to her surprise, like a pitcher full of clear, fresh water. She'd eaten all her breakfast without Mama saying a word to her and suffered through family prayers without one complaint that the Bible story was weird. But then Marylee was late stopping by for her and they'd had to rush and almost gotten to school late. And the English class had had a substitute teacher who was horrible and mean and said Louisa was talking to Susan, which was not true! By lunch she had become that pitcher of water, but only half full.

The afternoon had been worse. She'd forgotten to finish her math homework and Mr. Freeman had said flatly that she'd get an F for the day. Then on the way home Sara Louise, the missionary kid, had asked her to a party right in front of Susan and Marylee. She had wanted to say, "No, I'm only nice to you because my mother tells me to be. I don't like you, and I don't want to come to your stupid party." But she couldn't do that. She had told Sara Louise she'd have to ask her parents. But she was so embarrassed. The pitcher was almost empty: she *was being poured out.*

That night, with only a few drops of water left in her pitcher, Louisa had gone to babysit for the McMullen twins. Sometimes they got along just fine, but not that night. Just after Mr. and Mrs. McMullen left, the twins dirtied their diapers—*both* of them, *on purpose*—just to be mean to her. How do you keep from throwing two smelly, uncaring babies right out the bathroom window? When there's nothing left to give, how can you keep giving of your time, of your energy, of your self? How do you keep going when the pitcher's empty?

Yes, she had been a pitcher of water, poured out. No, she had been a pitcher of *blood* poured out. But when the blood was gone, she was not dead. She had to go on breathing, changing dirty diapers, gently putting two spiteful kids back in the playpen.

Two tears wet the corners of Louisa's eyes. She looked up. The preacher was still preaching. Mr. Henderson was frowning even though no one was laughing, especially not *her.* "Oh, God!" she sighed as a prayer. "I *am* like Jesus—blood poured out for this stinking world! Is this the way a Christian has to live—always giving, giving, giving?" The words of Mrs. Otis trumpeted in her head: Be like Jesus! Her mama's words thundered back: Be nice to

Sara Louise. She's been living in Zaire for the last four years and she needs a friend.

"Okay!" Louisa tried to quiet the voices in her head. Then she whispered, "I don't want to be poured out for others. I don't want to give till I'm empty inside—empty and dry."

Louisa sighed a deep sigh and looked at the empty communion table. She frowned, then looked to Mr. Henderson, but his face was hidden behind a visitor. "Maybe," she sighed again, "maybe the pinch of bread and the wetting my tongue with the wine are symbolic of God's filling us back up. Jesus' blood poured out from his big pitcher into my little one."

She liked that idea. "Then we ought to have communion every week, every day, every meal—because I need a lot of filling up. And so does my mom. She gets awfully exhausted and stressed out."

Louisa's mind was popping with ideas now: "But even if that's true—that God refills our pitchers—that's not enough. I mean, that's what I've heard all my life. God gives to us; we give to others. We give and give and give till the pitcher's empty and then some. Well, that isn't fair. I can't give what's not there! The God pitcher doesn't come around often enough. Yet people always seem to want more, especially Sara Louise. Something's missing."

Louisa relaxed after that mental outburst and looked again at the empty communion table. She started replaying in her mind that weird story they'd read in family prayers on Friday. "Let's see. It was about David . . . when he was fighting the Philistines. Goliath, the giant, was a Philistine, wasn't he? Anyway, the Philistine army was occupying the town of Bethlehem. And David and his men weren't too far away. And David was probably daydreaming the way I always do. David was thinking of Bethlehem and the well near the gate and the sweet-tasting water there and he sighed, 'I'd sure like a drink from the well in Bethlehem.' I know that's not the way David said it in the Bible, but that's what he meant. Three of his top fighters heard him and decided to slip out of camp, through the enemy lines over to Bethlehem, and they actually drew water from the well. Man, was David surprised when sometime later they handed him a cup of water and said, 'Here, here's what you ordered!' " Louisa thought that water would probably be as cool and taste as clean as the mountain water she drank from a spring on their last vacation in the North Carolina mountains. If she had been David, she'd have said, "Thank you," and drunk every drop. Maybe she'd have offered to share it with these three brave officers. But David poured it on the ground . . .

poured it on the ground,
and the ground soaked it right up.

That water was gone, disappeared—not even a wet spot like on the rug.

He poured it out—how had her father explained it?—as a drink offering to God. And he said something weird: that it was the blood of these three men who'd risked their lives, so he poured it out as an offering to God.

Water, blood, poured out to God.

But that's it, that's the missing piece: poured out to God.

That wasn't quite so scary . . . to be poured out to God. She didn't know exactly what it meant but she remembered an experience last summer at the Montreat Youth Conference. On the last day her small group had been given construction paper and colored wrapping paper and clay and string and pipe cleaners. And the leader had asked everyone to make something to give to God. Louisa had at first thought, How can I make something to represent my life? No, that's too vague. How about my future? I want to be a missionary or a nurse in order to serve God.

But that seemed too far away. Then she'd thought of Timmy. She'd liked Timmy a lot and thought he'd liked her. But he hadn't. Six months after they'd started seeing each other, after she'd fallen down during cheerleader tryouts, he'd started hanging around with someone else. Her heart still felt bruised when she thought of him. But she didn't want to give God her love, and she just did not like the boys she knew who went to church. She'd even told God once that she'd find her own boyfriends, thank you. God could have her life and her future but not her love. But maybe that was precisely what she needed to give God. So she had made a rose—a clay stem, green construction-paper leaves, a red wrapping-paper flower—like the one the Little Prince loved so dearly and left behind on his planet when he came to Earth. A single rose. And she'd given the rose to God. It hadn't been easy, but it'd been the right thing. And although she hadn't found a new boyfriend right away, she did discover she liked herself more, and she had met Susan. And there were two boys who were just friends, but she trusted them a little.

So here she was staring at the communion table. How would she give her life, her energy, her pitcher partially filled with water or blood to God? "Not first to others," she said to herself, almost vehemently. "First to God." But how?

Again Louisa sighed a deep, long sigh. "Communion is kind of a challenge to me to be like Jesus. Funniest thing, Mrs. Otis was right. I *am* poured out all the time like a running garden hose, like Jesus. And some of the time God wants me to be poured out for others. But the important thing for me now is to pour myself out to God or to give my being-poured-out to God, or whatever. How can I do that?"

She looked at her hands folded in her lap and in her imagination she held the communion pitcher filled with wine. In her fantasy she stood up and proceeded toward the table, bringing the pitcher as her offering. "God," she whispered, "this is my blood, my life; I give it to you."

Then her mind switched to the pitcher of water broken on the hall floor. "And God," she whispered, "this is me also. This is me, broken, spilled. I give my broken, spilled self to you. I'm scared. You know that, God. I don't want to be poured out. I want life always to be easy and good to me. So this is a new commitment, a new adventure with you, God. I don't know what this all means. But I want you to help me pour out myself to you first and then for others."

The preacher had finished the sermon. Hurriedly Louisa drew a picture on the back of the bulletin and stood a little late with the others to recite the creed. The service was almost over. After the benediction and the closing song, everyone started milling around. No one noticed as Louisa very reverently laid her bulletin on the communion table. On it was drawn an empty pitcher and the words, "Given to God. 6/14/87."

THREE

Narrative as Plot

ROBERT G. HUGHES

How do you measure the development of something as intangible as a narrative style of proclamation? What bench marks are there to chart progress?

When you cut down a tree, you clearly see a ring for every spurt of its growth. You couldn't see the tree growing. The rings, however, are evidence that it grew.

Before my wife and I wallpapered our kitchen the last time, in a dark corner on the wall, there was a series of light pencil marks. Every six months or so our boys insisted on being measured, and each quarter inch was a cause for celebration. You can chart physical growth that way, but how do you chronicle the development of a preaching style?

As I thought about that question I became convinced there was but one way: the path of autobiography, personal story plus reflection. As someone said, our lives are "stories with plots." The form must not betray the content.

For the reader's sake, however, I have attempted to organize my reflections, with headings that identify what I have come to regard as essential characteristics of narrative preaching.[1] Admittedly my list is neither comprehensive nor complete, since both genre and practitioner are very much in process. Incidents and insights have been disciplined to present themselves in more or less chronological order.[2]

I am comfortable with a first-person narrative approach. I think it's fun to reminisce and helpful to look back from some chronological promontory and see the route by which I've come. The starting point and the first few legs of the journey have dropped below the horizon. Reconstruction will be difficult, for I didn't take notes along the way. But exploring the attic on rainy days is therapy for me, and with luck I may find a treasure or two to share.

PERSONAL STORY

One of my earliest childhood memories is of Sunday dinners. These were wonderful occasions at our house, not only because we sometimes had steak (which did not grace our table during the week) and generous scoops of ice cream for dessert, but because my grandfather normally came to dinner. He lived next door and ate there during the week, but on Sundays he presided at the head of our table. These dinners were Pop Pop Bonschier's chance to shine. Conversation during dinner was limited to lighter matters, with the pastor's sermon of the morning the only exception to the rule. But when the main course had been disposed of and the dishes carried away, through dessert and long afterward, the resident historian for my mother's side of the family regaled us with stories of the way things used to be in community, church, and family.

There were times when fascination with the stories of a nineteenth-century mining town and a German immigrant family wore thin. Sometimes we heard the same stories four or five weeks in a row, and I prided myself in being able to finish the tales (silently) before my grandfather puffed his way to the end. Many Sundays I found excuses to slip away before the storyteller tired and withdrew to the parlor for a nap on the Morse chair.

But the narrative grew and developed subtly in the mind of a precognitive thinker. In time I found myself in and through the story.

My father's storytelling place was the back porch swing. He held forth there almost every night in summer, and often I joined him, usually after dark, when games of "hunts" and "tag" were over. As the rusty chains played their music in the dark, the history of my father's side of the family took on flesh and blood. Often in a confused way, my father's current joined my mother's to form a narrative stream. In that flow I found identity and purpose.

In retrospect I can see that the stories of my grandfather and father ordered my growing world.[3] As special narratives raised above the level of ordinary experience the developing Hughes saga helped one minor member of the clan to make sense of his life.

The time would come, in my adolescence, when I failed to appreciate the past and its complex of stories. I viewed my mental and emotional saga as primitive, rudimentary, a history I needed to grow beyond to find and be myself. Certainly I regarded that past as needing correction and perfection. Only later on did I realize how profoundly the dinner table and the back porch shaped my perceptions, determined my judgments, and guided my future course.

Not all the historians who influenced my childhood were family members. Sometimes the passing of the tradition fell to storytellers who, without even knowing it, impregnated impressionable youngsters with the images and lessons of local history and mythology.

"Not all that glitters is gold, fellows." The speaker was the wise man of our neighborhood, in that little town in the coal regions of Pennsylvania where I grew up. Harvey was the storyteller a couple of us boys went to on rainy Saturdays, when the ball field turned to mud, and there was little to do outside. His tall tales helped to pass the time.

"Not all that glitters is gold." Harvey said that all the time; it was his favorite expression. But on one particular day that axiom became linked to an object. With the rain pelting outside Harvey chuckled as he displayed for my friends and me a chunk of bright metal in his blue miner's handkerchief. Harvey had worked at the Number 14 colliery for thirty years before his retirement. It was in that dirty hole in the ground that he salvaged the glittering rock he exhibited.

For more than an hour Harvey regaled us with miners' stories. He spoke of Sutter's Mill, California, where in 1849 the most famous gold rush in history began. He spoke about men and women all over the new country who abandoned farms and homes to brave the deserts and mountains of the west to strike it rich in El Dorado, the golden land. He told of nuggets in crystal streams and seams so filled with the glittering metal that a miner could get rich in a week.

Then, with a kind of sigh, Harvey spoke of iron and copper pyrites that resembled the real thing in color and shine but were worthless. The cagey veteran's own nugget was probably a form of sulfur diamond common in anthracite mines. And even as he cradled it in both hands, Harvey was warning three wide-eyed nine-year-old boys that the rock wasn't worth very much at all. "Not all that glitters is gold."

Since that day when I was dazzled by a worthless rock in a miner's handkerchief, I've seen a lot of glitter that wasn't really gold. But whenever I see living examples of phoniness and sham, I picture Harvey cradling his sulfur diamond and mesmerizing three youngsters with tales from the gold rush of '49.

Some scholars argue that memorability is one of the least important functions of images, but that characteristic figured strongly in my encounter with Harvey and his stories. I retained much of what he said while the yarns of other storytellers were soon forgotten.

In both my preaching and my teaching of preachers I have come to link my experience with Harvey to an insight of Peter Brook's. When a play is over, the director notes, one thing is left:

> The event scorches into the memory an outline, a taste, a trace, a smell—a picture. It is the play's central image that remains, its silhouette, and if the elements are rightly blended this silhouette will be its meaning, this shape will be the essence of what it has to say. When years later I think of a striking theatrical experience I find a kernel engraved on my memory: two tramps under a tree, an old woman dragging a cart, a sergeant dancing, three people on a sofa in hell—or occasionally a trace deeper than imagery. I haven't a hope of remembering the meanings precisely, but from the kernel I can reconstruct a set of meanings.[4]

Clearly Harvey had a knack for focusing his stories on some object, some glittering rock, some picture that captured the essence of what he had to say. I retain so many of his tales and their attendant lessons now because the fit between narrative, image, and axiom was nearly perfect.

FAITH STORY

Besides being aids to memory, images also have a shaping function. I drew my faith identity from many of my experiences at St. John's Lutheran Church. Ours was the red brick church at the bottom of the hill, the "German Lutheran" as everyone called it, as opposed to the "English" church at the top of the hill. Years before, the Lutherans in Tamaqua, Pennsylvania, had split over the language to be used in worship, but that was ancient history. The few members of St. John's who still spoke German were viewed by kids my age as mild curiosities.

In the primary department of the Sunday school each class had its own space. These were not individual rooms, but at least a faded curtain separated rowdy boys from one another. In the third or fourth grade, however, you went into what we called the big Sunday-school room. I remember the room as very large, with chairs lined up like soldiers at parade for opening exercises, then circled up for individual classes.

That first Sunday in the big room, along with the size of the place and the incredible din of everyone talking at once, I was impressed by the banner or poster that hung above the stage area. This yellowed eight- or nine-foot monster, as I recall it, displayed a growing thing, something like a tree, labeled "The Christian Church." One set of branches bore the title Orthodox, another cluster was called Catholic, and still another Protestant. My memory is that the Lutherans had their own place right at the top of the Protestant cluster, and the Lutheran branches seemed to reach into heaven.

In retrospect I find the symbol and its provincialism humorous, but at the time that banner became a clue to identity for an eight- or nine-year-old. I used the banner as a memory hook for all the Martin Luther stories I came to know and love, and they in turn gave the image a narrative context. In time I perceived that I was a different sort of Christian from my friend Joe Davey, who ate fish on Fridays, wore a religious medal around his neck even when he went swimming, and went to school and church at St. Jerome's. He was a Catholic; I was a Lutheran.

I had found my place in the Christian story. During my years in the "big room," faced with the yellowed "monster," I accepted the religious view it represented. Years later in a seminary classroom I struggled to see myself and my church as part of the Catholic tradition. Emotionally I remained a top-branch Protestant for a long time, and in my struggle to reshape that vined symbol I gained a grudging appreciation for the power of images to label and shape.

Of course, my mother read Bible stories to me, and later on I read them myself without much prodding from parents. Many of the "bathrobed" saints of the Bible became my personal friends. I liked the Joseph stories, particularly the coat of many colors and the prison dreams. Samuel was a favorite, because the notion of God speaking directly was both appealing and fearful. Samson's muscles had as much appeal as the Charles Atlas advertisements in Dick Tracy comic books. Several friends and I spent an entire summer constructing and lifting "free weights" made from two gallon-cans filled with cement in an effort to destroy the temple and win the heart of the Philistine princess who lived two blocks down the street.

But in retrospect, it was not the reading of Bible stories or hearing them read in church or listening as they were dissected in the sermon that affected me most. The Bible really came alive when Pastor Gilbert Martin retold those stories with all of the color and energy of a former 245-pound tackle on the Muhlenberg College Mules.

That was not part of the Sunday morning routine; church with its vestments and processional was much too formal for storytelling. Rather, "Moose" Martin (as he was known in gridiron days) was a key figure in my years at Vacation Bible School. Along with the singing, Bible-story time was the part of "opening exercises" I liked best. After the entire school had assembled, and when the buzz of young voices had built to a roar, the bulky pastor would appear. His stomach protruded in front, and frequently his shirt-tail would be hanging out in back. But this ragtag appearance seemed to enhance the storyteller's mystique.

Biblical narratives were Pastor Martin's stock-in-trade. The room fell silent as his eyes took on a faraway look and he cleared his throat to call the "mob" to attention. As he warmed to his task

Pastor Martin began to pace and then to perspire. Biblical characters came alive. Kings drove chariots and Cadillacs, warriors used swords and bazookas, merchants hawked spices and bubble gum. I wonder now if our pastor was a fan of Peter Marshall and his "sanctified imagination." I have some sense of the pastor's style predating that of Frederick Buechner by several decades. But what I know for sure is that when Pastor Martin told Bible stories we kids could feel the centuries melt. We were there, on Mount Sinai with Moses, in the lion's den with Daniel, or in Gethsemane with Jesus.

I learned some things from Pastor Martin's rendition of the Genesis stories which I later needed to unlearn, about the creation of the world in six days, Adam's unnecessary rib, the origins of language, sin, and the pains of childbirth. But this etiological dimension of biblical narrative had little interest at the time. I know I absorbed some sense of biblical chronology, although even as a college student I wasn't sure if Daniel and the lion's den belonged in the Old Testament or the New. One thing is certain: when I got to the seminary no one needed to tell me that the people of the Bible came "warts and all." I remembered David's lust, Samson's monumental ego, and Paul's inflated sense of right and wrong. These people were real individuals who lived in my mind and imagination and with whom I could relate. Most importantly, I got the sense that God acted in human life, in the episodes of peoples and nations, and even in the lives of individuals like myself.

STRUCTURE

Improvements in the physical plant of St. John's Church—a new educational building to be exact—provided a seminal image for me of putting things together. That's because I spent one summer working for the contractor, the Schilbe Lumber Company, as their youngest and most inexperienced employee.

I'm afraid that the project was completed despite me. If you dig near the northeast wall of the auditorium you will find the wheelbarrow load of concrete I spilled. Just beneath the men's rest room is the pipe I punctured with one errant blow of my pick. The resulting gusher drew an *Evening Courier* photographer to the scene and I made page one. Later on, when Clem Schilbe was forced to declare bankruptcy, I felt partly responsible.

Nevertheless, that summer in construction gave me a sense of something substantial coming together. In the midst of a jagged hole in the ground foundations were laid, walls rose, floor and ceiling joists gave support, a roof was added. Something formless took shape. The building grew inside out, purpose dictating configuration first and appointments later on.

I know the arguments against using substantial images for sermon design, especially the danger of "construction" symbols with their suggestions of something solid, completed, and inert.[5] But when you work ten hours a day for the best part of three months, through a haze of sun and sweat, and you witness a building rise, the construction site becomes a delivery room where a living thing is born. In seminary, as I struggled first to shape stories and ideas into sermons, metaphors of design and construction spoke to me, because in my experience St. John's educational unit was a living thing.

So structure, with its construction images, had a place in my understanding by the time I took my first course in homiletics at the seminary. I smile today as I find my professor, Edmund Steimle, numbered among a dying breed of didactic preachers— the end of an era. To be sure, his preaching had didactic features, as does my own, but not in a dull or traditional sense.

Steimle's sermons did not begin with overt propositions. They had two points more often than three, and points were not enumerated in advance or along the way. I never had the sense that Steimle was arguing a case, at least not in the classic sense, or manipulating the rhetorical tools of persuasion. Steimle's messages were profoundly biblical, not topical, and he allowed the entire pericope to speak. Of course the professor's messages had didactic content; Steimle used theological language without apology. At the same time, my mentor had a sense of structure that moved from a description of the human condition to the response of faith, from law to gospel. One question was central to each sermon critique: What is the good news here? From Edmund Steimle I learned the law-gospel flow that, when crafted with sensitivity, is profoundly narrative.

A disconcerting sense of how essential it is to structure oral messages came in the early years of my parish ministry, in the mid-1960s. In those days Clyde Reid's *The Empty Pulpit* articulated the fears many of us had about preaching and its future.[6] But Reid's work was not simply a negative critique. He called for new ways to cut the psychological distance between preacher and people. On the theory that the physical and psychological are related, many of us, faced with congregations who shunned front pews and huddled as near as possible to the rear door, took to the aisles.

It was a fad that passed quickly, but I spent two years or more preaching several times a month from the midst of the people. With notes or manuscript in hand, movement and continuity were not primary concerns. I said what I had to say more or less in the order in which it occurred to me, and if I lost myself in that process, there was always the manuscript for reference.

That stream-of-consciousness period ended when I ventured forth without a manuscript. Suddenly, some sensible flow, either logical or emotional, became essential to me. Without it I could not remember the sermon. Sequence became a prime concern as, without my crutch, I looked the listeners in the eye, witnessed up close their glazed looks of confusion, and attempted with them to put the message together.

PLOT

A sense of plot began to develop in a college course on the short story. I was a literature major, so I did a lot of writing, primarily analytical papers. In the short-story course, however, my colleagues and I both studied and practiced the craft of "short fictions" (as the professor liked to call them). While we analyzed the work of Henry James, Ernest Hemingway, and Jack London, we struggled to craft our own stories. Late into the night, often lubricated by snifters of sherry in the professor's den, the six or seven of us struggled with the interdependencies of character and plot.

In short fiction there is no space for leisurely character development, extended philosophical musings, or the exploration of inviting bypaths. There is simply a story to be told. Character takes shape as protagonist and reader journey rapidly together from complication to development to resolution. I learned later that sermons provide similar constraints and possibilities.

Depth of plot did not come easily to me. My first story was about a boyhood friend we called "Noodle," in recognition of his pointed nose. As I read it now, twenty-eight years later, I would argue that while my friend Noodle did take on flesh, at my pen he never really breathed. This Pinocchio-like figure tested nothing, had no insights, neither grew nor changed. Noodle was a pasteboard figure lacking values, realistic struggles, and discernible motivation.

In his analysis of the English novel the literary critic and novelist E. M. Forster summarizes the difference between story and plot.

> We have defined a story as a narrative of events arranged in a time sequence. A plot is also a narrative of events, the emphasis falling on causality. "The king died and then the queen died," is a story. "The king died and then the queen died of grief," is a plot. The story answers what happened next; a plot tells *why*.[7]

Using the Forster definitions of story and plot as my standard, I would say that I did fairly well with "what happened," developed a sense of sequencing events in my later experience of aisle preaching, but I struggled profoundly with "why?" The multilevel, directed interaction of character and situation that leads to insight—the guts of successful fiction—is what I identified as a challenge years ago and continue to list on my present agenda.

It was years after college graduation—when two of my sons were nearly grown—that I received another real insight about plot. My third son, David, at about twelve years of age, discovered the *Choose Your Own Adventure* books, which are stories designed to involve the reader in an unusual way. The stories are not structured to be read one page after the other in numerical order. Rather, at the bottom of nearly every page are instructions on what to read next. The reader seems to skip around a lot, and must frequently make choices. "If you decide to call the police and report a possible murder, turn to page 65. If you decide to come back later and sneak up on the house from a different direction, turn back to page 15." What happens in the story depends to a large degree on the reader's own choices. How does such a story end? Some of my son's books had twenty or more possible endings from which to choose.

Sermons provide a similar opportunity for listeners. While we preach "our sermons" congregational members put their own together on the spot. They plot their own stories. While we go on preaching, listeners often reflect or even daydream. Even when people stick with the preacher to the bitter end they are forced by the apparatus of perception-cognition to construct their own meanings. Helpful sermon models will assist them by providing alternatives and directions.

For example, Matthew 13 says, "The kingdom of heaven is like treasure hidden in a field, which a man found and covered up; then in his joy he goes and sells all that he has and buys that field." The preacher might begin by asking a baffled congregation what the parable intends. Is Jesus an expert in money management, a financial high roller, advocating that we get involved in highly speculative land deals? Not likely! Is the parable maker an expert in developmental psychology, urging that we risk all in pursuit of inner dreams that shape our lives? Maybe we ought to do that, or maybe just sometimes—we pause to puzzle over current possibilities. At the same time the preacher will go on to the real subject of the parable, something Matthew calls "the kingdom," God's rule. Most likely Jesus was challenging first-century listeners to risk everything on the rule of God in their lives. A preacher today would attempt to leave twentieth-century listeners, if they have taken the entire journey, with the same challenge.

The rhetorical manuals might label this a "ladder" sermon if, step by logical step, it proceeded from A to C, from land deals to God's rule. Years ago, preaching in a didactic mode, I would have gotten to the kingdom in the first five minutes, would have taken seriously only that option, and would not have invited listeners to explore alternatives.

As a preacher with growing narrative inclinations, I struggle now to craft messages that engage listeners emotionally as well as cognitively, draw them into a struggle with issues, and assist them to move from where they are to a point where they are free to respond to the gospel. As I become more adept at constructing plot lines rather than arguments, I assist listeners to choose their own adventure, and in that process to discover and experience God's rule in their lives.[8]

COMIC MOVEMENT

The sense of a person's life as a narrative plot moving from tragedy to hope came home to me when my grandfather died. I had been away from my hometown several years when Pop Pop died, so his funeral services became a time to reconnect as well as to conclude. After the viewing, close relatives went back to the homestead to talk it through alone. There in the midst of my grandfather's personal effects, with most of the family present, we laughed and cried together as we painted a "portrait" of the person we loved. From the stories that came, the good and the not-so-good, the jovial grandfather and the temperamental shopkeeper, emerged a narrative of a life's journey.

The motif of passage was acted out for me in the funeral procession the next day. I was to be a pallbearer for the first time. I learned years later that bearing the body to the grave suggests the movement of the person out of this world, but I felt that long before I knew it. Struggling to lift a heavy casket into and out of a hearse, stumbling through the Odd Fellows Cemetery to the family plot, and seeing my grandfather lowered into an earthen grave with prayer and benediction gave me a sense of passage. A phase of life had ended; something new was beginning—for all of us.

In later reflection I became convinced that it is the structure of the entire funeral rite, together with the words spoken, that enables the grieving, the giving up of the dead, and the reinvestment in life. The deceased, prepared and prayed over, moves to another mode of existence, while the survivors reform their lives and pass on to a new phase of life here. The entire event was redemptive for me, because it communicated in visible and spoken terms the Christian gospel of life over death.

Dan Via introduced the duality of Aristotle's tragic and comic into the study of parables.[9] The tragic plot, said Via, is one "moving downward toward catastrophe and the isolation of the

59

protagonist." The comic plot, however, is one that "moves upward toward the well-being of the protagonist and his inclusion in a desirable society." Thus the Book of Job becomes comedy, not because it is funny, but because the plot moves from tragedy to hope. Jesus' parable of the Prodigal Son moves from "death" in the far country to "joy" in the father's house.

It is characteristic of the Christian plot that the tragic is a prelude to the comic.[10] In the midst of the death/life contradiction of our daily experience, the movement is upward toward hope. In reflecting now on the funeral of my grandfather, the reality of the tragic was affirmed in the committal of his body to the ground. Simultaneously, in the midst of death there was proclaimed and enacted the good news of life.

The comic movement from law to gospel, from death to new life, the movement that Steimle taught homiletically, I internalized at my grandfather's grave. I continue to regard the presence of this "good news" as the litmus test of Christian preaching. Assisting students to plot this movement in preaching Christ crucified and risen remains my primary agenda as a teacher of preachers. What this pattern looks like in practice will become clearer from the sermon that follows.

NOTES

1. I continue to accept the conviction of Edmund Steimle that the image of the storyteller is formative for preaching since it both articulates what preaching is and frees people to do it. Steimle postulated that preaching is shared story involving the juxtaposing and interweaving of the biblical story, the preacher's own story, and the story of the congregation. That essential definition is stated in various ways and developed by Steimle, Morris Niedenthal, and Charles Rice in *Preaching the Story* (Philadelphia: Fortress Press, 1980). This book was seminal for me as I groped toward an understanding of the type of preaching I had been struggling to do for most of my ministry.

2. As I thought about the writing of this essay, my intuition was that after twenty-five years of ministry I was already in touch with most of the experiences and related insights that were formative in my development as a preacher and teacher of preachers. If that were the case, it seemed to follow that many of these narratives and insights would be prominent in

my sermons and lectures. That instinct proved accurate, as a search of my files led to one rediscovery after another.

3. Ian Barbour defines myth as "a story which is taken to manifest some aspect of the cosmic order." That is how my grandfather's and my father's stories functioned for me. See Ian Barbour, *Myths, Models, and Paradigms: A Comparative Study in Science and Religion* (New York: Harper & Row, 1974), 29.

4. Peter Brook, *The Empty Space* (New York: Avon, 1968), 124.

5. I agree with the critique of architectural images for sermon design by Thomas Long in *Preaching Biblically*, ed. Don Wardlaw (Philadelphia: Westminster Press, 1983) 85–86, but for me St. John's educational building was experienced in narrative fashion "over time."

6. Clyde Reid, *The Empty Pulpit* (New York: Harper & Row, 1967).

7. From E. M. Forster, *Aspects of the Novel* (1927; reprint, Harmondsworth, Eng.: Penguin Books, 1962), 93–95.

8. What Fred Craddock labels "inductive movement" in his classic *As One Without Authority* (Nashville: Abingdon Press, 1971) I call "narrative plot." Narrative preaching shares its essential dynamic of tension-complication-resolution with all storytelling.

9. Dan O. Via, *The Parables: Their Literary and Existential Dimension* (Philadelphia: Fortress Press, 1967), 110, 145.

10. Northrop Fry, *Anatomy of Criticism* (Princeton: Princeton University Press, 1957), 215; quoted in Via, *Parables*, 146.

From Ashes to Alleluia

Text: Gen. 3:19

This sermon is typical of my style. Further, it displays characteristics of narrative preaching and relates to events in my development already described in the essay.

The heavy use of personal narrative was planned to allow the listeners, who did not know the "guest preacher" personally, to identify with me and my background. I knew in advance that some members of the congregation had roots in my home area. Of more importance, most of the older persons present had grown up with coal-fired furnaces and their ash residue, making the controlling image a familiar one.

It was not the practice of St. John's to impose ashes on Ash Wednesday, but one purpose of the sermon was to assist these listeners, in a "cool" atmosphere, to begin to rethink the significance of the image and its liturgical function. A specific goal was to give the practice a broader Christian context to prevent it from being rejected as simply "Roman" practice.

The style of the "script" is one person's attempt to bridge the gap between written preparation and oral speech. Clusters of material separated by white spaces may or may not be grammatical paragraphs. Sentences are grouped to aid the preacher to keep them together in delivery. Punctuation marks suggest the length of pauses, with periods indicating full stops. White spaces between clusters mark protracted pauses.

Ash Wednesday,
with its dirty smudge on the forehead,

evokes a host of memories for me.
Ashes are a part of my life story.
Can that be true of some of you as well?
I grew up no more than fifty miles from here, in Tamaqua,
a community surrounded by ashes.
My father mined coal for a living,
and we were proud to have a coal-fired furnace in the basement.
From the time I started school
it was my job to take out the ashes.
Remember those days?
What slid down chutes into the basement, hard, wet, and black
came out gray and soft.
In summer I removed big tubs of ashes on my wagon.
In winter a sled became my truck.
When the tubs were dumped over the bank at the rear of our
    house
I came in gray from head to toe.
Ashes and dust mark our lives.

Ashes and dust flank the story of Adam and Eve as well.
The narrative in Genesis 3 says that it was out of dust, from ash,
that the Lord God formed the man
and breathed into his nostrils the breath of life.
Adam came from dust to become a living being.
As long as the first couple trusted and obeyed their Creator
life went well for them.
But then there was that awkward incident with the snake.
In this ancient story eating the fruit of a special tree
would have made our forebears wise . . . like God.
They were tempted, they ate,
And they knew that they were naked.

Life changed in Paradise for our ancestors . . . and for us.
They were young and full of life, but they felt naked.
They were at home in the garden, but they were exposed.
They were God's own creatures, but they knew guilt.
Sin and rebellion sent them hurrying
to the nearest outlet store for clothes,

to hide their shame from each other . . .
and from God.

Do you remember God's word of judgment on them?
"In the sweat of your face you shall eat bread
till you return to the ground, for out of it you were taken;
you are dust, and to dust you shall return."

Dust at the beginning of life,
dust at the end.
On Ash Wednesday, dust is a graphic reminder
of God's judgment on sin.
Of course, the words of Gen. 3:19
carry a message even more sobering than their reminder of sin.
The text speaks also of mortality, yours and mine.
"You are dust, and to dust you shall return."

Not too many years ago
only Roman Catholics got ashes on Ash Wednesday.
I recall my confusion when I first saw the dirty smear.
Mom had a hard time explaining why it was
that kids who went to St. Jerome's got ashes
and kids who went to public school got nothing.
It was in our seminary chapel, no more than five years ago,
that I received ashes for the first time.
We came to the rail one by one
where ashes mixed with olive oil were applied to foreheads.
Looking me straight in the eye Professor Krych said,
"Remember that you are dust,
and to dust you shall return."[1]
Finally I had it, but I wasn't sure I wanted it.

When you and I most enjoy life,
when faces brim with smiles,
when hyacinths push yellow heads through soft earth
as harbingers of spring,
Ash Wednesday interrupts with its gloomy message,
"You too shall die."

A devotional writer put it this way:

What fire does in an instant,
time is always doing to everything that lives . . .
all this flourishing life, turns to a little ash,
a handful of dry dust which every wind scatters
this way and that.
Everything to ashes. Everything!
This house I live in, these clothes I am wearing,
my money, my property, the dog that follows me,
this hand I am writing with,
these eyes that read what I write,
all the rest of my body,
people I have loved, people I have hated or been afraid of,
whatever was great in my eyes upon the earth,
whatever small and insignificant,
all without exception will fall back to dust.[2]

A tub of ashes on a child's wagon,
a word spoken to our parents,
a smudge on a damp forehead,
all reminders of sin and mortality.

But wait a minute. Wait just one minute!
In the early church, ashes and dust
were also symbols of repentance that leads from death to life.
Have you heard the expression "sackcloth and ashes"?
When the Christian church was young,
as early as the fourth century in Rome,
the imposition of public penance became an official rite.[3]
People removed from the church for serious public sin and scandal,
but people who wanted to be restored,
approached their priests shortly before the start of Lent.
In turn their priests presented them before the bishop of the place.
These public sinners were given a uniform to mark them off
as persons wanting to amend their lives,
garments made of the poorest cloth,
ashes on their heads.
Today is called Ash Wednesday,
because on this day sackcloth and ashes set people apart
who were on the road from death to life.

Repentance, you see, is not a process devised to embarrass us.
Repentance is not public shaming at the hands of a vengeful God.
To be sure . . . there must be a willingness to come before God;
there must be a humbling before the throne;
there must be an honest admission of sin and guilt.
But most of all . . . repentance is being turned in our tracks;
repentance is responding to God's living tug on our lives;
repentance is God's good news.

Even growing up with Roman Catholic friends,
I never understood what the smudge on the forehead signified.
By the end of a school day the dust
was smeared and blurred by sweaty palms.
I know now that the ashes are applied in the shape of a cross.
The God who reminds us of sin and mortality,
"you are dust, and to dust you shall return,"
is the same God who sent Jesus to destroy both enemies.
On the cross Christ gave his life to break the power of sin.
On the cross Christ died to overcome the power of death.

In Denmark, when a body is committed to the ground,
as earth is cast on the coffin,
the pastor sums up life's journey;
"From dust you were created.
To dust you shall return.
From dust you shall rise again. Amen." Alleluia![4]

NOTES

1. *Lutheran Book of Worship: Ministers Desk Edition* (Minneapolis: Augsburg Publishing House/Philadelphia: Board of Publication, Lutheran Church in America; 1978), 131.

2. Romano Guardini, *Sacred Signs* (London: Sheed & Ward, 1956), quoted by Philip H. Pfatteicher in "Meditation On Ash Wednesday" (Philadelphia: Commission on Worship, Lutheran Church in America, 1973).

3. Francis X. Weiser, *Handbook of Christian Feasts and Customs* (New York: Harcourt, Brace & Co., 1958), 174–75.

4. Pfatteicher, "Meditation."

FOUR

The Narrative Quality of Experience as a Bridge to Preaching

EUGENE L. LOWRY

"A really fine job," my mother said. It was October, 1952, and this was my very first homiletical experience. I was grateful for her warm post-service greeting. Then she added, "although it sounded a little bit like a debate." A debate? Little wonder. I was a sophomore in college and had just been appointed as a student pastor in the Methodist church. When I moved behind that pulpit, I walked straight from the debate chamber. Since early in high school, I had been involved in debate programs and, besides playing the piano, debating was my chief avocational interest.

At the time I thought I had pretty well mastered the principles of public speaking in general and of intercollegiate debate in particular. I knew how to make a case. I understood the principles of outlining as well as other techniques of moving toward an inescapable summary. It mattered little what the debate subject was, or whether I was speaking for the affirmative or negative side of the issue. The structure was clear.

Indeed, it had been clear since the very first speech course I had taken. During preparation you move toward the articulation of one propositional sentence that states unequivocally the theme you are going to address. In the speech itself, you begin with an introduction that identifies for listeners the exact subject to be covered. The theme is divided into three Roman-numeraled parts and is restated in a conclusion.

As I understood it, the big difference between utilizing such principles in debates and in pulpit work was in the selection of "evidence." In the debate hall evidence consisted of hard data that would undergird the thesis. In the sermon, "evidence" tended to be less formal—even a folksy anecdote could be utilized. Soon I found myself purchasing several volumes of popular anthologies of sermon illustrations which were as handy for filling out the outline as the concordance was for selecting the text for the already determined theme.

In either case, the presentation was deductive in form, with the conclusion announced in the introduction, divided and particularized into the three-point body, and then reiterated in the conclusion. In the pulpit you had one extra chance: if in doubt, you could always close with a prayer and, hence, summarize it again.

This homiletical form was not only familiar to me because of my prior experience in debate, it was congenial to my temperament: I never spoke before my mind was made up. And long before I became familiar with the Shannon-Weaver Construct, I had it well-nigh perfected: the art of communication consisted primarily of transmitting a set of complete ideas from one location to another via the "conveyor belt" called speech. A formal speech essentially was a conveyor belt moving only in one direction.

My seminary courses in preaching did not significantly alter my understanding of a speech or a sermon. As I understood it, the purpose of preaching classwork was to hone the craft, expand the sources of illustrative material, and deepen the theological content of the propositional theme. Yet, in terms of structure the explanations in *The Principles and Practice of Preaching* by Ilion T. Jones[1] were not much different from those made by Sandford and Yeager in *Principles of Effective Speaking*,[2] a popular text for speech classes.

I remember very well my great surprise to hear Ronald Meredith, the new pastor of First Methodist Church, Wichita, Kansas, preach. He seemed not to follow these long-used methods of preparation and delivery. I was so impressed with his style of preaching that I wound up serving on the staff of that church—primarily to find out what it was he did and how.

To my great sorrow, I discovered that he didn't *know* what it was that he did—or how. In fact, he expressed surprise that others did not do the same. Ron Meredith was a good storyteller; his illustrations were magnificently told. I was able to learn from him how to better handle illustrative material. But the principle of sermon formation that he utilized remained a mystery to me during those three years of ministry. Apparently, it remained a mystery to him as well. Yet, I sensed that his charisma was not limited to his manner of speaking, although that was quite remarkable. His charisma also had to do with how the content was formed. But whatever it was, Ron did it intuitively. Hence, one could only stand back in admiration—even awe.

Of course, such a posture of admiration—or envy—had the chief function of causing me to admit that while he could do it, I could not. It simply was not "who I am." No one had ever accused me of being a storyteller. Seldom could I even repeat a good joke. Nor was I a spinner of family yarns.

Upon reflection, I suppose it should be noted that many people, perhaps most, can do something they are unable to explain in principle. Certainly, I could not explain how it was that at the age of five I could climb on a piano bench and repeat my older brother Ralph's piano lesson. Actually, I did more than that—I would add a flourish or two not written in Thompson's *Primer*. All I knew was that I could do it. It made Ralph quite irritated and it made me very happy—a lifetime of motivation thus came into being.

By the time I stepped behind that pulpit for the first time, I had become rather adept at piano improvisation—and I still did not have a name, let alone any articulated principles, for it. But at some point, I was surprised to realize that the connection between Ron Meredith's sermonic form and my piano improvisation lay in a great deal more than the fact that neither of us knew quite how it was that we could do what we did—that both of us were functioning with an intuitive skill without corresponding articulated principles. The truth is, both *his preaching and my piano playing were based on the principles of narrative form.* Had either Ron or I been familiar with Aristotle's *Poetics* at that time, we would have been able to name precisely what it was that we were doing.

What I consider most peculiar in all of this is that although I was applying these principles of narrative form at the keyboard, I could not do the same in the pulpit. At the keyboard I was a participant in a narrative art form; at the pulpit I was a deductive, thematic preacher. Through the years my preaching has had little impact on my piano playing. My piano playing, however, has utterly transformed my preaching.

Although Aristotle was talking about literary form when he spoke of the plot moving from opening conflict into complication through *peripetia* (reversal) toward denouement, he just as well could have been discussing—before its time—the dynamics of jazz improvisation. The connection between the two was recognized by jazz historian and professor Leroy Ostransky. He wrote, in *The Anatomy of Jazz*, that "what distinguishes superior creative musicians from the mediocre ones of all periods is the manner in which they create resolutions, and to create resolutions it is necessary to set up irresolutions. . . . Poor and mediocre jazzmen will impose problems on themselves, problems of resolution whose answers are already evident in the irresolutions they set up. . . . Jazzmen in these categories often do not understand that the quality of their jazz will depend not on any resolution, however elaborate, but rather on the inherent intricacy of the irresolution."[3]

Regardless of the artistic depth of power of a jazz musician, the principle is the same. You begin with a fairly uncomplicated melody line, chord structure, and beat, and through improvisation turn it into complication. You allow the rhythm of the melody line to "get sideways" with the meter rhythm, deviate significantly from the melody line, and begin adding more complicated chordal moves. Things become so complicated that very shortly the untutored ear scarcely can recognize the tune. When several musicians are working together, the different moves of several instruments complicate matters further until the musicians themselves begin to press toward a kind of boundary: their minds begin to concentrate on the question, How now are we going to get home? Sometimes when a less accomplished musician is working with other more sophisticated musicians (as would often happen when I sat in for an absent piano player) the more naive musician may in fact get lost from the other members of the group, not quite understanding what is happening with the group, where they are at that moment, or where they are heading.

The successful turn toward home often comes as a surprise, with the musicians making turns they could not have anticipated before they began the number, and with negotiations that likely can never be repeated. Generally the song is completed with a final chorus that becomes a return to the fairly uncomplicated original melody. Musical denouement it is.

The phrase "return home" will not come as any surprise to preachers within the black tradition. Every black preacher understands that for the sermon to happen, it must move to a final celebrative event—a denouement. Again, there is no coincidence in all this, because, in fact, jazz improvisation grew directly out of the black preaching experience.

It was the homiletical improvisation of the black preacher, together with the contrapuntal participation of the congregation, which developed into jazz improvisation in the first place. No coincidence is it either that in early jazz circles the trumpeter—the lead instrument—often was called "the preacher." When James Wendell Johnson first sought a title for the work we know as "God's Trombones," he called it "Trumpeters of the Lord." There is even a 1939 Louis Armstrong recording that includes a verbal introduction to the music in which he says: "Sisters and brothers, this is Reverend Satchmo getting ready to beat out this mellow sermon for you. My text this evening is 'When the Saints Go Marchin' In.' "

The connection between lead trumpeter and preacher is not the only perceived link between these two art forms. Performing similar roles were such blues singers as the great Bessie Smith, probably the best known of the early blues singers. As one listener explained, "If you had any church background, like people who came from the South as I did, you would recognize the similarity between what she was doing and what those preachers and evangelists from there did."[4] It is particularly strange, then, that I would have been following narrative principles at the keyboard (without knowing it), while at the same time preaching nonnarrative sermons. Indeed, my transition toward narrative preaching happened over a span of years, yet long before I found the term "narrative" to define it. Had someone told me that I was moving toward becoming a narrative preacher I would have thought it nonsense. Certainly I was using illustrations, but the sermonic structure clearly was topical.

I believe what happened was that my use of illustrative material began to spill over on either side of the illustration. In particular, it began to dawn on me that there was an enormous difference in listeners' attention during an illustration and before it or after it. As a result, I began to utilize a different kind of illustration, moving from a momentary anecdote to an extended story. Rather than making a point and then illustrating it, I began to allow the story to carry the freight by making the point itself. Finally, the obvious dawned on me: often Jesus's preaching was simply one long story. Yet, even then I would have said, "I'm no storyteller. I don't tell jokes or spin yarns."

Then, in 1970 I was preaching a series of three sermons in a special preaching event away from home. I happened to utilize a parable of Jesus as my text for the evening. After the service a man greeted me and said, "Fine story." The next evening's sermon also happened to be based on a parable of Jesus, and after the service this same man clasped my hand and said, "You're not so much a preacher as you are a storyteller." I took his comments to be complimentary, but hardly could believe them to be true. My final sermon, as I had planned it, did not have a narrative text. Very quickly I shifted to another parable of Jesus. I went home musing on this new perception of what was happening to my preaching style. It began to dawn on me that whether preaching a narrative text or not, in sermonic form I was moving from problem to solution, from itch to scratch, in virtually all my sermons. The fairly simple problem/solution format became more detailed, and my "homiletical plot" was born.

Even then, however, I had not made the connection between my music and my preaching. It was only after I came upon Aristotle's writing that I began to discover what my piano playing had been doing to my preaching. In particular, it dawned on me that both music and preaching are temporal events, not constructions of space. Whether in speech preparation or sermon development, I had been organizing my material. I cannot imagine a musical composer conceptualizing the work as "organizing" the composition. The development of any musical theme always involves the "imagining" of a future acoustical event.

This is because music, whether manuscript or improvisation, happens in time. It is a temporal event or it is nothing. The musicians' work comes into a musical envelope out of silence and returns into the mystery of silence's time (as Michael Williams has phrased the matter in the context of story). In between the silences, the key to good jazz improvisation is the risking of increased complication in order to prompt the surprising turn home—just like Aristotle's conflict, complication, *peripetia*, and denouement. In nonimprovisational musical form the same complication is planned, such as in Mozart's famous adaptation of "Twinkle, Twinkle, Little Star." When this process happens well, it is as though the musicians had heard Oliver Wendell Holmes say, "I wouldn't give a fig for the kind of simplicity which exists on this side of complexity, but I would give the world for the simplicity that exists on the other side of complexity."

In retrospect it is clear to me that it was my intuitive skill at the keyboard—in particular, the increasing complexity moving through the surprising turn toward resolution—that instructed me, albeit unconsciously, about narrative preaching.

If it is true that all of life is interconnected, and if British critic Barbara Hardy is correct in her claim that all of life is lived in narrative form—indeed, that the web of story is the fabric of human existence—then surely it must be true that other people may be able to draw from other kinds of endeavors that are narrative in form, as I have drawn from music. For instance, my brother Ralph never could improvise at the keyboard, but at a very young age he would dismantle unworkable clocks and motors and then put them back together again. At the time, I was absolutely amazed that although only a piece or two would be at the root of the problem, he would take the whole apparatus apart, even undoing pieces that were working exactly right. In the middle of the project he would have what seemed like a thousand pieces out on the table. I was certain he had crossed the boundary into chaos and that the small problem was now a very large problem. But somehow he found the simplicity on the other side of complexity— and the fool thing would work once more. His fix-it process was as clearly narrative in form as my piano playing. While Ralph had his hands on a clock and was working from simplicity to complication to transformed simplicity, my hands were on the keyboard, attempting the same thing.

Sometimes while moving toward increased complication in musical improvisation, a performer will make a musical blunder, will, for example, inadvertently reach for exactly the wrong note or chord. A good musician will turn the mistake into a phrase never even imagined before. Sometimes this narrative mistake will become the most important facet of the performance—with other musicians in the group building on the accidental turn. Microbiologist Alexander Fleming while doing ongoing bacteriological research made a comparable blunder. Inadvertently, he allowed mold into the container that held the culture of bacteria. The stray mold killed the bacteria with which Fleming was working. Instead of throwing the culture away—as lesser scientists might have done—he was immediately curious as to why the mold killed the bacteria. His mistake coupled with his curiosity resulted in his discovery of penicillin. Such surprising turns, whether experienced in scientific endeavors, jazz improvisation, or in simple, everyday tasks, are central to that longer narrative journey called life.

It is crucial to note here that although many of us may not see ourselves as narrative preachers—believing firmly that such preaching is not for us—we may be surprised at our narrative skill in other endeavors. For Ralph, it was fixing clocks and motors; it could just as easily be quilting, skiing, carpentry, cooking or skateboarding. My hunch is that if we explore other activities that we do reasonably well, we will discover two things: first, that such skills, hobbies, or sports, when analyzed, may likely reveal narrative shape; and second, that the sense of narrative form that emerges can, by analogy, be applied to one's practice of preaching.

I am convinced that had someone asked me to name what I do in piano improvisation—that is, to state the various ingredients and processes of the event—and then had named it for me as narrative form, I long ago would have made the connection and could have moved toward narrative preaching intentionally. Even if someone had heard me play the piano and then said, "Now, do that homiletically," I would have known what to do in a very short time. Without that crucial power of naming, it took me years to bring together these two different behaviors. Simply stated, I had to wait until it happened to happen.

THE CONCEPT OF GIFTS

Behind all this discussion lies an important conviction about *gift, knowing,* and *learning.* People involved in all forms of art—even those persons as limited in talent as I—grow accustomed to the well-intended remark: "Well, you certainly have a gift"; or, "No one can teach you that." Such remarks are intended as compliments, and hence the proper answer is "Yes, it is a gift; thank you." Of course they are correct. Artistic temperaments, capacities, and sensitivities are given to some. When I first walked up to the piano and imitated my brother's music lesson, I had no musical training whatever. I had a gift. Yet such a statement is only half true—at best.

But sometimes in response to a gift-remark, a person wants to respond: "Yes, it is a gift—plus fifty years of work." The problem behind such remarks as the artist hears has to do not so much with what is affirmed explicitly, but with what is denied implicitly. What is denied overall is that others can get what you've got, as if a capacity can only drop out of the sky, as it were, complete and whole. You "either have it or you don't." The truth is that such gifts are not nearly so rare. John Elliott, with whom I study harmony and theory, teaches all kinds of students, some with a long history of improvisation, some with traditional musical training, and some with no prior musical background whatever. Several of his students never "played by ear" at all prior to his teaching. While capacities or aptitudes sometimes seem to "drop out of the sky," other times they are fashioned in ordinary skill-training endeavors. What we call gifts often can be taught to a wide range of people.

Consequent to the either-or mentality regarding *gift* is the apparent denial that artistic aptitude be analyzed for the purpose of identifying variables. This may be of a piece with the view that art is devoid of cognition, or at least conception. My contention, epistemologically, is that art of whatever form does indeed involve knowing, and that although the form of knowing may be labeled aesthetic, gestaltive, or "right-brain" knowing, it is available for discursive or linguistic analysis. The fact that some exceptionally talented people may not be able to name what they do may only mean that because of their extraordinary talent there simply has not been adequate need or occasion for such analysis. The use of analogy (as suggested above) is a particularly effective way to learn how to name the variables of "natural" talent.

That art forms are in fact taught suggests that art is not grasped only intuitively and in no other way. Indeed, any good art instructor will tell you otherwise. To be sure, art instructors are grateful for whatever gifts and aptitudes the student brings, and will even encounter some would-be students who can be helped only marginally. But the good instructor knows that the teaching process must be geared to naming the "intuitions"; otherwise, even the highly gifted cannot be developed a great deal. Learning an art form emerges not as a process of clustering learnings around or building on natural aptitudes; it is the naming of the natural aptitudes themselves so they can be developed and enlarged. In other words, *learnings* and *natural abilities* are not two separate genres of skill. Learning does not stand outside or alongside a native ability. Learning is a self-conscious disciplining of the native ability so that the gift itself grows.

My harmony/theory instructor would go further by noting the extra difficulty of assisting those who have been working on their gifts without professional assistance. Indeed, shortcuts born of natural ability and experience often impede artistic growth. Jay McShann is an immensely gifted jazz pianist. Indeed, many years ago he became nationally known as a blues player. He could not read a note of music. He was, however, not simply gifted; he was very smart. He interrupted his career to take music lessons, to learn the notes and the theory behind his playing. His artistic capacities at the keyboard expanded in geometric proportions. He is now regarded as a legend in his own time. Those with the "gifts" do well to study what it is that they do naturally in order to develop the art. What we call a gift usually refers to a cluster of variables not yet named, and hence falsely perceived as unreachable, unknowable, and unteachable. The truth is many others can learn what a few seem to inherit.

Hence, my recommendations to those who are fairly convinced that narrative preaching is not a personal, live option for them are two. First, engage in a personal inventory of other skills and aptitudes related to work, hobbies, leisure activities with a view toward discovering the narrative components of these processes. Second, compare those narrative components to narrative-preaching theory in order to discern connections, parallels, and analogies of the homiletical art.

Certainly philosopher Michael Polanyi is right in saying that we know more than we can tell. Yet, sometimes we cannot do until we can tell what we already know.

NOTES

1. Ilion T. Jones, *The Principles and Practice of Preaching* (Nashville: Abingdon Press, 1956).

2. William Phillips Sandford and Willard Hayes Yaeger, *Principles of Effective Speaking* (New York: Ronald Press, 1942).

3. Leonard Feather, *The Book of Jazz* (New York: Meridian Books, 1959), 151.

4. Leroy Ostransky, *The Anatomy of Jazz* (Seattle: University of Washington Press, 1960), 83.

Strangers in the Night

Text: John 3:1–9

The streets were dark and deserted.
Not a soul could be seen—at least he hoped not.
There *was* one lonely figure—jumping from shadow to shadow—
   never using the major streets of the town,
   traveling only in out of the way places,
   hoping not to be seen.

So, what's he doing, jumping from shadow to shadow in the middle of the night?
   He is going to pay a call on Jesus who is staying with friends in the village.
   He doesn't want anybody to know that he, one of the leaders of the community, would be going to see this itinerant preacher.

Jesus is roused from his sleep, I presume, and meets Nicodemus.
Strangers in the night.
   "Rabbi, you must come from God," Nicodemus says,
   "because nobody could do the signs you do except God be with them."

To which Jesus responds, "Truly, I say to you, unless one is born anew, one cannot even see the Kingdom of God"
   —and right away it strikes me that we have a communication problem here.

Did you sense the opening greeting and the response do not quite compute? . . . Let's go through it again.
"Rabbi, you must come from God, because nobody could do the signs you do except God be with them."
"Truly, I say to you, unless one is born anew, one cannot even see the Kingdom of God."
Strangers all right; strangers missing in the night.

And I must say I am a bit shocked at Jesus.
Wouldn't you expect Jesus to respond to Nicodemus's compliment with at least a gracious "Well, thank you"?

I mean, the minister is greeted by a parishioner on a Sunday morning with, "Preacher, you must have been inspired today, for nobody can preach the way you preached except God be with them."

I hope the preacher will respond, "Well, thank you so much," or, at least, "How long did it take to figure that out?"
I presume the preacher will not respond with, "Well, it *is* almost two hundred miles from Des Moines to Kansas City"
—which is the truth of course—but what does that have to do with the previous comment?

Actually the opening greeting and response are not quite as unrelated as they first appear. And were we Jews in the days of Jesus, we probably would have understood.

For centuries there was a set of norms by which would-be prophets were judged. One had to have had some visionary-type experience, have engaged in prophetic proclamation.
What Nicodemus was saying was that he had added up the score, and concluded that, indeed, Jesus was a genuine, A-1, guaranteed prophet of the Lord.

Jesus' response is simply, "No, you can't get here from there."
One does not add up the score of understanding and arrive at the conclusion of faith.

No, it is the other way around. Only those within the circle of faith are able to discern the evidence.

Of course we know that from our own personal experience. Have you ever tried to argue someone into the Christian faith? Just answer one argument and three more will follow.

> The Sunday school teacher was trying to be creative on Easter Sunday morning, and said to the class, "What do you suppose is the first thing Jesus did once he was raised from the dead?" To which one of the class members responded, "I'll bet he really told Pilate off."

No, he didn't tell Pilate off—he appeared only to those already within the circle of faith.

> "Rabbi, you must come from God because. . . ."
> "No, unless you have been born again you cannot even see the Kingdom."

Well, unfortunately, Nicodemus was not much of a poet—couldn't get the hang of the *metaphor*—and with literalist blinders on said, "But, I am old. How can an old man reenter a mother's womb?" (Or as Frederick Buechner has put it, "At my age I have trouble getting into a cab—let alone a womb!")

So, while Jesus is trying to evoke the Word, Nicodemus is stuck on anatomy. "The wind blows where it will. You don't know where it comes from and you don't know where it's headed, but you can hear the sound of it"—and feel the breeze across your face. To which Nicodemus responds, "How can this be?"

Poor Nicodemus. . . . But it's not a bad question.

"You must be born again." I never did like the phrase myself—and I remember it all too well from my childhood.

> Our family often traveled across western Kansas to see the grandfolks. I would peer out the rear, side window—with nothing to see. Absolutely dull out there except when, all of a sudden, a set of Burma-Shave signs would break in with a message of cheer.

But then we would come upon one of those large billboards—obviously the work of amateurs—and it would declare,

"Ye must be born again."

Seemed kind of pushy to me.
Why didn't they mind their own business?
  "You must be born again?"

I never like the phrase and, for that matter, never really understood what it meant—until several years ago when I ran into Fred again.

Actually, Fred is not his real name, but his name for today. Fred is a close friend of mine, but across many miles. I don't get to see him often, but we always pick up where our last sentence left off.

Fred is a minister, too.
  He didn't go to the same seminary as I did.
  Quite a bit younger than I: too young to be my brother, and too old to be my son.

Now, Fred is a winner—
  the sort of person who could sell anything to anybody.
  Looks like a young corporate executive.
  By this time probably drives a BMW, with a bumper sticker on it that says, "Go for it."
  He always has—and always wins the prize.

After seminary Fred moved to a state where United Methodists abound. He moved right into a suburban setting, and in only a few years in that church he
  doubled the membership,
    tripled the budget,
      and was a terrific success—except around the house.

I remember how his first wife used to wait until he was a few steps away. She'd lean over toward me and say,
  "I know you have a lot of influence with Fred.
  Do you suppose you could get him to relax?
  Maybe take a half-day off each week?
  He does nothing but work."

Of course I tried—gave it my best shot—even asked him what he wanted me to say at his funeral—but without result.

Things went so poorly at home that finally Fred and his wife went their separate ways. Their divorce got the attention of the cabinet right away. The bishop decided he would take care of Fred.

He fixed him all right: sent him to a much smaller congregation where there was little chance for the kind of success he'd had before.

And of course, a great reduction of salary.

So, when we happened onto each other at a meeting, Fred suggested that we have lunch together. And we did—the three of us: Fred, his new wife, and I.

Right away Fred told me about all the wonderful success he was having at the new church—success beyond the fact that there he had met the woman who would become his new wife.

The budget had already nearly doubled,
    attendance had more than doubled,
      a big building campaign was being considered.

Then Fred told me how unhappy he was. Not anything wrong with the congregation—they had been very responsive to his leadership.

"I'm just restless," he said.

While we were eating, Fred spotted someone he hadn't seen in a while, and excused himself to go say hello—which left me sitting with his new wife. She leaned across the table and said:

"I know you have a lot of influence with Fred. Could you do me a favor?

Could you get him to read?"

Well, it was almost the same request as his first wife had made—perhaps more on target.

Apparently, she sensed something lacking inside . . . and thought that reading might help.

I don't mean intellectually—Fred is very bright;

I don't mean lacking in devotion—he is committed;

No, it is another kind of "lack."

It was while driving home from that meeting and lunch that I realized precisely what was amiss.

It is an existential emptiness . . . and with a different kind of guilt. Guilty—not of anything he has done or failed to do—yet somehow guilty of never being who he really is.

It was Nicodemus who came to mind as I drove home that day. Somehow Fred revealed exactly what was Nicodemus's problem . . . or was it that Nicodemus revealed exactly what was Fred's problem?

Do you remember when Jesus started talking about being born anew? Do you remember Nicodemus's response?
He started asking what *he* had to *do*.
"How can an old person climb back into a mother's womb?"

"What do I have to do?" That's his question.
"What do I have to do?" That's Fred's question.
"How much success is required?"

You have to be born again, Jesus said—
which is precisely that which one can *never* do,
no matter how committed,
how hard working,
how bright.

The one thing no one can ever do is to birth oneself.
Birth is always a gift of another.

Poor Nicodemus,
jumping from shadow to shadow to get the last word on precisely what he had to do to make it right.

Poor Fred,
running from success to success, seeking the triumph that finally will bring home the prize.

Poor John Wesley,
riding on his weary horse from campaign to campaign, hoping to achieve that peace he had sought for so long.

And all along, that which is sought so desperately is available
without price,
without achievement.

You must be born anew, said Jesus, and announced the good news
of the gift by declaring that:
The wind blows where it will.
You can't control it.
You can't work for it.
You don't even know when or where or how.

The wind blows where it will,
and you can hear the sound of it,
feel its breeze against your face . . .

unless, of course,
you are running so fast,
and with the jaw set so desperately
that you can't hear anything,
feel anything, . . .
not even the grace of God's spirit.

Which is to say:
Nicodemus, give it up; stop trying so hard.
Fred, give it up; success will never secure it for you.
Sharon, give it up. . . .
Allen, give it up. . . .
Martha, give it up. . . .
Gene, give it up. . . .

The wind blows where it will,
the gentle breeze of God's unconditional love.
And that's a promise,
a promise made to every stranger in the night.

FIVE

The Samaritan Parable as a Model for Narrative Preaching

WAYNE BRADLEY ROBINSON

If someone had asked me when I was fifteen years old, "What do you think of preachers?" I would have answered, "Just keep them away from me!" I had rarely been to a worship service in a church of any kind and, when I had, whatever it was that the preacher was saying seemed either incomprehensible or boring. My other encounters with "preachers" had been on the street, where I had been accosted many times with the "mini-sermon," "Have *you* been *saved*?!" I knew that my older brother had saved me from drowning once, but other than that, I didn't know what they were talking about. And from the threatening way they were talking, I did not want to know any more about it, at least from them! All in all, preachers and what they did had little appeal for me. Webster's definition of preaching seems to fit what I had come to know of it: "to exhort in an officious or tiresome manner."[1]

Then, some friends urged me to attend a summer conference sponsored by the New York Conference of the Congregational Church. My resistance was overcome by the promise from my friends that there would be a lot of good-looking girls there and that it would be fun to be on a college campus for a week. Also, I figured that I could avoid those sessions that involved having to listen to preachers. But once I got there, I became caught up in what was going on. And much to my surprise, not only did some of the preachers seem to make sense, they seemed to be amazingly decent people. Looking back on that week, I realize that it brought about something like a conversion in me.

When I got home, I started attending the nearby Congregational church. Some months later, I was sitting on my brother's bed by myself one afternoon, trying to figure out what to do with this new (to me) "religion business," when I had the incredible sensation that an invisible but tangible yoke was being placed on my shoulders. And there were words that seemed to go with it: "*You* are to become a minister/preacher." I didn't know what to make of it nor how to respond. It was certainly not something that fit my expectations for myself up to that point. Nor was it something that my parents would have thought about for me. At first, I told no one about this experience. And when I finally told my girlfriend, I started with, "You probably won't believe what happened to me; I'm not sure I do, but. . . ." When I got up the courage to tell my parents, they did not know quite what to make of it. So they invited the minister of the Congregational church over to "have a talk with me (us)." His basic advice was, "Go ahead and do it only if you cannot do something else!" He meant, I think, that I should be sure that this is what I wanted to do more than anything else.

Over the next several years, I struggled with the idea of becoming a minister. By now, part of me truly wanted to do that. But an even stronger part had many doubts. On the one hand, I had real questions about my gifts matching up with what I knew about what ministers did, especially preaching. On the other, I wondered about that moment in my brother's room, about whether I was deluded.

In December of my sophomore year of college, I had another of those luminous moments. I have seldom talked about this particular experience, partly because I had never had this kind of experience before and partly because of the reactions of others when I have shared it. But the experience has remained such a key part of my journey into ministry in general and such a crucial part of my search for a liberating, noncoercive preaching style, it seems important to share it in this context. The experience began with me praying, as I had so many times before, about the core issue of whether God really wanted me to be a minister/preacher. This time I felt urged to pick up my Bible. When I did, it fell open to a page I could not remember having read before, and these two sets of words stood out:

You shall worship the Lord your God,
and God only shall you serve.

and

The Spirit of the Lord is upon me,
because God has anointed me to preach good news to the poor.
God has sent me to proclaim release to the captives
and recovering of sight to the blind,
to set at liberty those who are oppressed,
to proclaim the acceptable year of the Lord.

(Luke 4:18–19)

This experience should have been enough, I suppose, but it was a measure of my self-doubt at that point that I decided to pick up my roommate's Bible, which fell open to that same passage with the same words standing out. I then went next door, borrowed a friend's Bible, and the same thing happened. By that time, I was convinced that I was intended to get some kind of message from this. Some months later, I had a ring made to honor this "event," and I have worn it ever since. On one side is engraved a closed Bible, on the other, an open Bible. In the middle is a symbol of the Holy Spirit. It was intended to symbolize what I had come to believe was the core of my "calling"—to help make it possible for the Bible to become a transforming resource in the lives of others, as well as to find ways for that to happen in my own life.[2]

But just how that was to happen was as yet unclear. For one thing, the force of those early "preacher" experiences lingered on. One was the unpleasant choice of the "street-preacher" style, which seemed so abusive. I was turned off by the underlying message of that style, which seemed to be "I'm OK, but you're hopeless." Another, the "lecture mode," did not seem to offer much more. It seemed to be an "I've got it, you don't" style of preaching, especially when it was combined with a moralistic type of appeal—"This is the truth, therefore you should." . . . So neither offered much promise of helping me envision preaching as facilitating the kind of transformation I had read about in the

Lukan text. Most of the preaching to which I had been exposed seemed to be indifferent, if not outright bad, news. Then there was always the possibility of doing preaching in some setting other than ordained ministry. On top of that, my college courses in Bible seemed to be making the Bible itself more and more of a lifeless artifact. Much the same thing happened at seminary. Most of the models of preaching to which I was exposed there did not offer much more promise than what I had experienced before. And, while I now knew a lot more *about* the Bible, how to use it as a transforming resource still eluded me for the most part. As a consequence, when I sought ordination I was still very unclear about how I could preach in a way that satisfied my hopes for that activity. I was also not sure about what to preach. So, instead of entering parish ministry right away, I decided to go on to get a Ph.D. in New Testament. Maybe then I would be ready to preach, I thought. After completing my doctorate, I entered parish ministry, partly because I had run out of things to study for which my parents would help me pay! And I did not want to go into teaching at that point. I did have a somewhat better fix on the "good news" itself, which was a great relief, but I still had many unanswered questions, including the pervasive "how" questions.

The responsibilities of preaching every week and helping laypeople prepare to teach Sunday school intensified my uneasiness. The "prophetic" mode so popular in seminary seemed suited to the big issues of the day—the Vietnam war and racial justice. But somehow I did not feel any more comfortable with being a "critical-parent" style of preacher than I had been when I had been on the receiving end of such a communication style. And I did not see much transformation coming about as a result of my preaching either. There had to be a better way of preaching and teaching. Some of the questions I sought answers to were: How do people learn best? How do people change? What facilitates/impedes such transformation? How do you move from examining Scripture to its examining you? Is the understanding of "the human" implicit in the "scientific" study of Scripture adequate? If not, what is? And what do you do with that?

To try to answer those and similar questions, I started an intensive study of the behavioral sciences, while keeping up with my biblical work. Over the next ten years, a method of working with Scripture in a new way gradually emerged.[3] For my purposes here some of the characteristics will suffice. They are:

1. An understanding of the human that includes the affective, volitional, and unconscious as well as the cognitive aspects of the self
2. Within the cognitive aspect, the conscious inclusion of right-brained as well as left-brained thinking
3. An inductive/Socratic approach to the study of Scripture
4. Conscious and careful utilization of these and other questions, insights, and methods borrowed from the behavioral sciences to enrich and supplement the historical critical methods I had learned.

By now I was feeling considerable satisfaction with the experience of developing and "field testing" a method of group Bible study which did unleash the transforming power of the Bible in people's lives. I had seen people make important and wholesome changes in their lives as a result of this style of encounter with Scripture. But I had not yet discovered something comparable in my preaching. I kept getting good feedback on my preaching, but *I* was not satisfied. I had tried the brainstorming/Socratic approach that had worked so well in small groups within my congregation as a whole, but it did not provide the answer I was seeking. However, that was soon to change.

In the summer of 1975, Herman Ahrens, the editor of *Youth* magazine, approached me to become a regular contributor to the magazine. The first piece I wrote, which became in approach the model for all that followed, started its life as a sermon. The original sermon began with my attempt to get ready to preach on Palm Sunday. It was about seven o'clock on Saturday night and I had already written over half of my sermon. But the sermon read as if it had no energy to it at all. I decided to go back to the Markan text and read it in Greek, just to see if that might not kick off something fresh for me. As I read, I came to the word *polos*, and thought, "If someone asked me to go get a *polos* (colt), I'd come back with a young *horse*." Then I saw the disciples were asked to bring back an *unbroken polos*. Having grown up around horses, I had a feel for what this might mean. I started to get a picture of Jesus as a kind of Lone Ranger, riding with tremendous energy and intentionality into Jerusalem. So I checked to see if *polos* could in fact mean young horse. I found that it not only could, but that this was indeed its normal usage. When it stood alone, it meant the off-spring of a horse. When it was used in conjunction with the name for another animal, it meant the offspring of that animal. So the event as reported in Mark had become radically obscured by what we find in Matthew, where Jesus has his disciples get not just one *donkey*, but *two*. From there other insights arose from a careful scrutiny of the text. I scrapped my other sermon, and the next morning I simply narrated, in condensed form, what I had discovered the night before. And I ended by saying something like, "I'm not sure what this all means, but here are a couple of my hunches about that. I'm sure you can add some more." Without realizing it, I had stumbled upon one way to do narrative preaching—to re-create one's journey of discovery with a biblical text. But I had not yet grasped that idea clearly.

The next day, I called Herman Ahrens to tell him what had happened and to suggest that this could become a challenging article. He agreed, and asked me to write it up and send it in. But when he got it, he called me and said, "What happened? When you told me about this, you were full of energy and excitement. What I have here is a lifeless piece of pedantry. On the phone, you sounded like an investigative reporter tracking down a fascinating story. How about rewriting it just that way?" So I did. This time, I got another call. "This is great, but what might the implications be for today? If we were to take this seriously, how might we act differently?" So I wrote a new conclusion to do just that. Were I to write it today, I'd change some things, but basically it became clear to me then that I had found at least one inductive/narrative sermon form that would do many of the things I had been searching for.[4]

The feedback that I got from this sermon, as I gave it in my church and as it appeared in print, seemed to confirm that I had in fact discovered a qualitatively different way of preaching. For one thing, it was noncoercive in its form. I was not stating a thesis at the outset to which I was asking assent, and then proceeding to "prove." People went with me on a condensed form of a journey that I had previously gone on myself. When I got to the ethical implications at the end, they were like discoveries we made together which impacted on me as much as they did on my listeners. In response to the sermon people said things like, "Wow, if this is true, then . . ."; "I didn't know Scripture could be so powerful!"; "The Jesus you talked about seemed so real and so challenging!" It was as if a piece of leaven had been put into the dough of people's lives, including my own! I felt as if I was finally getting a handle on how I could develop what I would later come to think of as the narrative style of preaching. Most of the subsequent articles I wrote illustrated how that style changed and developed for me.[5]

As I worked on this new form for preaching, several things helped me expand my understanding. One was Fred Craddock's book *As One Without Authority*, the first book I had read which named, undergirded, and expanded on many of the things I had been working toward. But as I look back on it, of even greater significance for me was my decision to look again at Jesus' own preaching, especially at his parables. As I looked at the parables as a preaching model, it struck me that traditional preaching is modeled more after *secondary* material than *primary* material. We had majored in the explanation style of the secondary material rather than the story form of the primary material. As Craddock said, we had become like backward joke tellers, putting the punchline first. Actually, I think that we were more apt to explain the "funniness" of the joke and never get around to telling it at all!

A NARRATIVE SERMON MODEL

Since my primary model for narrative preaching comes from this work with the parables, I would like to turn to one of those now— the parable of the Samaritan (Luke 10:29–37)—to show what happened. The sequence in that parable starts with a question, "Who is my neighbor?" This is a real issue, and one with which we all wrestle at one time or another. We all have to decide every day whose needs we are going to respond to and whose we are not going to respond to. For a minister, this is an especially acute issue. I can think of many people in my congregation whose needs as my "neighbors" could conceivably take precedence over the word processor in front of me! How do I decide? Jesus! I could use some help too!

Identify the Issue

In the case of this parable, we have a fairly obvious clue to the issue. In the traditional sermon model, if there was an issue, it was resolved in advance. "This is the answer" to your question, whether you have asked it or not. But my model starts with the question (to myself): "What is the issue?" Something has to be "up in the air."

But finding the issue that is the key to the rest of the sermon is not always easy. This past summer, for example, I wrestled with the lectionary text, Romans 9:1–5. Prior to that text, Paul has just finished with the lyrical passage about the tenacity of God's love (Romans 8). Then he says abruptly "Truth, I now tell you in Christ, I am not lying" (9:1). At first, I thought the issue in these first two verses was "truth." So I did a lot of work on this issue. But that did not seem to have any life to it. So I tried to restate the issue. Maybe it is "How to be a believable person"? So I worked on that for a while. But that did not seem to be it either. Then I wondered, what had happened in response to which Paul "comes on so strong"? It seems that somebody in Rome had spread a story about Paul which was different from his understanding of what had happened. So the issue was: What do you do when you hear back a story about your behavior that you know to be false? In the sermon itself, I chose to start by telling a story about a time when that had happened to me. So, step one in the model becomes: find a way to state or image the issue without moving to its resolution.

Explore the Issue

The next steps seem to be designed to heighten and dramatize the issue: details are artfully chosen. In the Samaritan parable the man was stripped naked—Would you want to be seen touching a naked man? He was beaten, presumably with visible marks of that beating—What if he has something broken? That first-aid training was so long ago. And he was left "half-dead"—If we read this last detail with a beginner's mind, we might chuckle to ourselves, "Which half is dead, which alive?" But this is the way moral choices are often presented to us. The options are such that it is truly hard to decide what to do. And even though touching a dead person had more formal negative consequences for a first-century Jew, most of us can still empathize with someone who does not want to touch a body. In exploring the issue, this kind of consideration is important. It is also important to note that no one in the parable is called "good," and no one is called "bad." It is a sign of our own moralizing tendencies that we have labeled the parable as that of the *Good* Samaritan.

The first person who appears in the proximity of the "half-dead" person is a priest. It is important to remember that he is not described as "bad" (nor is the Samaritan described as "good"). There was considerable anticlerical sentiment in the first century, which probably helped shape this story in its original form, but there were nevertheless good reasons for the priest not to want to risk touching the "half-dead" man. The priest was probably on his way back from a week of demanding service in the temple, away from his family. He was probably, much like myself after a Sunday service, suffering from an overload of people's demands and expectations, and his compassion was nearly all used up. If the man were dead, and the priest touched him, he would have been barred from religious service for life. And when he got home, he could not have touched his family members for a considerable period of time because he would have been "unclean." Much the same set of issues would have affected the levite, except that he would have not been barred from service for life. Besides, both of them may not have been feeling well. In the normal diet of that time meat was a rarity, but in the temple, the priests and levites ate mostly meat (from the sacrifices), from which many of them became ill.

At this point in the story, a Jewish listener would have expected a Jewish layperson to appear, because other current stories followed in that pattern. But the Samaritan appears instead. The word "Samaritan" had at least two translations: the first, rooted in the Samaritans' own sense of identity, came from *shamerim*, "the observant ones." In other words, they were as bound by the cleanliness laws as were the other (observant) Jewish people. The name *Samaritan* also meant, for those who looked down on them, the *shomeronim*, "those people" who live in Samaria, the half-breeds. Because the one who acts compassionately is a Samaritan, the listeners are forced to begin to reframe the issue, and to move in unexpected directions. In this model, we have begun to move from the second part, exploring the issue, to the third part, reframing the issue.

Reframe the Issue

At this point two directions are available. In terms of identification, the original listeners had to make an unwelcome choice. They probably would not have identified with the priest or levite. This left the "half-dead" man, with whom they would not likely have identified before. And choosing the Samaritan posed problems. We also have to "get in the ditch" with the wounded man or identify with the Samaritan. If we choose the Samaritan, the question arises, How was his experience different from the priest's and levite's? I suspect that a Samaritan would not have gone to Jerusalem, except for some need that overcame his fear of being mistreated there. Perhaps he had to go there to trade goods. Most likely his experience in Jerusalem would have been a wounding one. A Jewish person was not bound to help a Samaritan in trouble and could lie to and cheat a Samaritan without pangs of conscience. Here, then, are two ways to reframe the "neighbor issue." One is to look at the probably hurtful experience of the Samaritan and say, "The clue to neighborliness is one's experience of being wounded like the Samaritan (that's where his ability to feel deeply, in his "gut," or literally, bowels [*splangchnidzomai*], came from)." The other is to look to the "ditch person" and say, "The clue to the neighbor issue is a willingness to look at one's experience of being ripped off, abused, and stripped 'naked,' and being helped by someone with whom you normally wouldn't even associate." Either way, the issue starts to become reframed. The reframing is completed by Jesus' question, "In your judgment, which of these three became a neighbor to the one who fell among the robbers?" (*my trans.*), and by the answer of Jesus' questioner. The original issue is never resolved as such. Instead, we have a new issue and a clue to its resolution. Stated succinctly, the reframed issue is, How can I become a neighborly person? And if I have heard Jesus' clue correctly, the answer is that the wellspring of compassionate neighborliness and the exercise thereof come from one's wounded self, not from one's conscience.

Resolve the Issue

The fourth part of the model has to do with the story's implications. In a sense, we have already moved into that part. In the original parable, this was probably left up to the creative imagination of the listener. The instruction to "go and do likewise" was probably added on by an early preacher, and as such it is worth thinking about. When I mulled it over, something that happened in my experience came to mind. A colleague of mine in another church was telling me about her experience there as a recently called minister. She described how lonely she felt and how hurt she was by the "constant criticism" she was getting. She asked me what I thought she could do. I suggested that she could let people see how much she was hurting and give them a chance to help her. Her reply was, "Oh! I couldn't do that, they'd eat me alive!" What she was saying was, "Those Samaritans would make sure I was not half, but wholly dead!" I subsequently preached at her Installation service. When it was her turn to speak, she found it so difficult that she cried. When she did, the people from her church who were on the platform with her immediately moved toward her and put their arms around her. And, having noted the body language of the others present from that church, I believe they would have done the same if they had been on the platform. The good news seems to be that it is acceptable to let our wounds surface, both as a source of or guide to our own compassion for others, and as a means of asking for help when we need it. So, "go and do likewise" is acceptable as a conclusion of this parable *if* it is heard as an empowering encouragement to use our deepest selves as our guide to behavior. But if it is heard as a moralistic appeal to conscience, "You should . . . ," then, as I understand it, it reverses or renders superficial the intended outcome of this parable/narrative sermon. So, to reiterate, the four parts of this model are: identifying or imaging the issue; exploring or heightening the issue; reframing the issue; and resolving the issue.

RESPONSES TO
NARRATIVE PREACHING

Several years ago, I was invited to speak at a meeting of the Minneapolis Ministerial Association on the topic of narrative preaching. The core of that presentation was the exploration of the model contained in the Samaritan parable, much as I have just done here. The response was very encouraging to me. Recent seminary graduates said that they had heard of narrative preaching, been drawn to it as an option, but had not "gotten a handle" on how to do it. This model, however, was one they could, and intended to, use. Many of the older clergy said that they had never seriously considered narrative preaching as an option, but having seen this model, they were going to try it. In fact, several of them later called me, as they were trying it, to bounce ideas off me as they worked. This feedback, along with that of my preaching students at United Theological Seminary, has been very encouraging, and has led me to believe that this is indeed a workable model that can be used by a variety of people.

On the other hand, I have also encountered criticism of the narrative style of preaching as not serious or not honoring the results of scholarship. Apart from the irony of this kind of charge (in view of the fact that Jesus himself used the narrative style), I believe that we do need the resources provided by scholarship to do this kind of preaching well. I find them indispensable as tools for probing scriptural texts and as an antidote to eisigesis. It is important, however, to use scholarly resources imaginatively and selectively. Very often this means supplementing the use of commentaries with other material. In the case of a parable, such as in my model, it is important to understand all the concrete details. These details are often overlooked by commentators as if the "point" were of primary significance, and the story itself simply a secondary, dispensable vehicle (a kind of modern-day mini-Docetism). One of the most available and comprehensive resources for getting at the significance of the concrete details is the *Interpreter's Dictionary of the Bible*.[6]

It is clear to me that narrative preaching, like any other mode of preaching, can be done either responsibly or irresponsibly. And it may be especially tempting to shirk from the effort necessary to do narrative preaching well: the research needed to do this type of preaching is often more time-consuming than that needed for the older style.

In conclusion, I hope that I have encouraged you either to try narrative preaching or to try a different way of doing it if you have not used the models presented here. For me, one of the most encouraging things about this way of doing preaching is that there are a number of valid ways to do it: we each can work out what is best for us.

POSTSCRIPT

Following the inductive flow of this paper, I turn now to some of the assumptions or conclusions that have "happened" along the way for me as I have worked on narrative preaching. These are not intended to be exhaustive. Rather, they are initial attempts to look at some of the issues. In each of these, there is a spectrum, at one extreme of which we have close to a caricature of the lecture mode and, on the other, the narrative mode.

Being . . . Becoming. In the lecture mode, emphasis tended to be on doctrines, ideas, and definitions. In the narrative mode, emphasis is more on process. The key process question is, "How does something work itself out in a life situation?" There is an exercise that helps one get a feel for this spectrum. First, pair off with another person and then ask each other three times (each time with a different answer), "Who are you?" Then repeat the process with the question, "Whom are you becoming?" Finally, reflect on that experience together. The answers to the first questions usually yield things like static roles, have little challenge and interest to them, and are past-to-present oriented. The answers to the second question usually are more challenging and interesting, and have a present-to-future orientation. I see the former as similar to the Greek way of thinking, the latter as similar to the Hebrew way of thinking. Another way of putting it is that the former "majors" in nouns, the latter in verbs.

Deductive . . . Inductive. In the deductive approach, the "truth" to be discussed, illustrated, or proven is stated at the outset. In the inductive approach, "truth" is discovered as the narrative unfolds, usually near the end of the sermon.

Original Sin . . . Original Goodness. Phillips Brooks once said that we have to decide whether people are basically children of God on whom the devil has laid a hand, or whether people are basically children of the devil whom God is trying to rescue. That basic choice, in one form or another, informs everything that one does in a sermon, from the flow of it, to the tone of voice used, to body language. Are we trying to help each other awaken our memories of our true (good) selves, or are we trying to "beat the hell" out of our listeners?

Logic . . . Imagination. The lecture mode in its extreme form implies that left-brained thinking, that is, reason, is central. From this flowed the emphasis on information and the reliance on stating a thesis and then backing it up. This implied change model presupposes that if people are better informed, they will act better. It is as if the realm of God would arrive if all people had Ph.D.'s. In the narrative mode, the emphasis is more on right-brained thinking, what I believe the Bible means when it refers to the heart. To have a hardened heart is to shut down one's authentic self and to shut out God. This does not mean that the narrative mode is "anti-intellectual," nor does it exclude left-brained thinking. It does, however, reflect a more complex view of the human and a more complex understanding of change. It is no accident that "imagination" is an extension of the word "image" (of God?). Webster's definition of *imagination* is in itself worth pondering: "the act or power of forming an image of something not present to the senses and never before wholly perceived in reality; creative ability; ability to confront and deal with a problem."

Authoritarian . . . Invitational. In the lecture mode, wherein conclusion is placed ahead of development, it is often assumed that the preacher had a right to expect assent from passive listeners at the very outset of the sermon. This is not as blatant as when "street preachers" claim this right, but it is just as real. The motivational approach is often to use "should" and "ought" and "must," as in "you should (I already do!)." The preacher resembles a critical parent chastising naughty children. In the narrative mode, the inductive flow itself invites the listeners to "take the journey" with the preacher. It is like one friend talking to another. In fact I often advise my students to imagine saying what they have to say as if gathered around a kitchen table with a few valued friends. This does not mean that there is no power in the latter mode. If this were true, Jesus would have affected no one.

Self-veiling . . . Self-disclosing. When I was in seminary I got the message that when I went into the pulpit, my identity was not significant. I should never refer to myself or to my experience. I was there as God's anonymous servant. As an antidote to "bragging," this might have had some merit. But it is simply honest to reveal one's thoughts in any form of communication. There are healthy ways to use one's own experience. One is to use one's personal experience with others. Another is to use one's own struggles with an issue, or stories where we are the antiheroes, not the heroes. Overall, I believe that we are simply more apt to trust and believe someone whom we can see has struggled as we have or who has had experiences similar to our own, than we would someone who will not disclose such struggles or experiences.

Abstract/General . . . Concrete/Specific. The lecture mode tends to deal in broad concepts. One sign of this was the word-study approach to Scripture. While there is value in this, it tends to reinforce the tendency for preachers to get lost in concepts and generalizations. As I often tell my students, everybody is nobody, but somebody can be everybody. For example, instead of the Samaritan parable, Jesus could have talked about the typical person who gets into trouble, how people are just so apathetic today, how they just don't seem to care. But I doubt if anyone would have remembered what he said, much less have been inspired to respond to it.

NOTES

1. *Webster's New Collegiate Dictionary*, 8th ed.

2. It is not easy to precisely define what I mean by "transformation." I see it as a shorthand definition of the kinds of impact made on people as described in the passage from Luke 4. Beyond that, we can point to its meaning by saying that we seek from Scripture something quite different from what we seek from encyclopedias. We go to the former primarily for inspiration, nurturing, and challenge; we go to the latter primarily for information. We usually hope this living encounter with Scripture will help us move into a healthier relationship with God, others, ourselves, and our world. In other words, I would hope that this encounter would have a transforming/shaping/liberating impact on our lives. This same impact is what I would hope for from the sermonic unfolding of the Word.

3. See my *The Transforming Power of the Bible* (New York: Pilgrim Press, 1984), in which I explain in detail the "new way" of working with Scripture.

4. The completed version of this sermon on the "triumphal entry" can be found in appendix 2 of *The Transforming Power of the Bible*, 215–20.

5. A compilation of many of these articles, plus others, can be found in my *Questions Are the Answer* (New York: Pilgrim Press, 1980).

6. *Interpreter's Dictionary of the Bible*, 5 vols. (Nashville: Abingdon Press, 1962–76). Other readily available resources that help us get inside the daily life of first-century Palestine include Joachim Jeremias, *Jerusalem at the Time of Jesus* (Philadelphia: Fortress Press, 1969); and Bruce J. Malina, *The New Testament World: Insights from Cultural Anthropology* (Atlanta: John Knox Press, 1981). I hope to pursue this issue more extensively in the future because I believe we must look more carefully at how exegesis has to change to undergird narrative preaching.

Angels, But Satan and Wild Beasts!

Text: Mark 1:9–15

I suspect that most of us, even if we are not inclined to take an interest in sports, were touched during the Olympic Games in Calgary by the story of Dan Jensen and his family. Here was a speed skater who had trained and trained and trained, as all Olympic athletes must, and had a chance at a gold medal, trying to skate a race while knowing that his sister, a mother of three children, had just died of leukemia that morning. Jensen fell in his races, the five-hundred meter and the thousand. There, before all the world, was the agony of not just Dan Jensen, but of his family and friends. It seemed almost too much to ask anyone to bear. As a local sportswriter said in effect in his column, "Why, God? Why couldn't this young man have at least one medal—something to remember his sister by?" And I am sure that many of us asked the same sort of question.

Dan Jensen's story reminded me that we human beings seem to be fated to wrestle constantly with the question, Why do bad things happen to such good people as the speed skater and his family? They seem to have done all the right things. We are told that they are deeply religious, close-knit, and very supportive of one another. They have been living exemplary lives, yet bad things happen to them. It doesn't seem fair. It does not make sense, and we want it to!

Among God's creatures we humans seem to be singled out, not

to have to face bad things—for they happen to other animals as well—but to ask why. Why do bad things happen, especially to those who seem to have done nothing to deserve them? A part of us at least wants good behavior to be rewarded by God and bad behavior to be punished by God. Then it would all make sense. It is no wonder then that this issue pops up over and over again. Just when we think we've got it resolved, it comes to plague us again.

In a Peanuts comic strip, for example, Linus is sitting on the floor sucking on a bottle of something as Lucy goes by. As she passes, Lucy says emphatically to him, "Nothing that is going on in the world today is my fault!" In the next frame, she walks on with a sour expression on her face, while Linus looks puzzled. But he recovers and says, while holding his bottle in the air, "I'll drink to that!" In another Peanuts comic strip, Sally comes in and announces to Charlie Brown, who is sitting in the bean-bag chair, "Don't blame me! That's my new philosophy!" Charlie Brown replies, "I thought your new philosophy was, "Who cares?" She then says, "Who cares? Don't blame me!" He responds, "What do I know?" To which she replies, "I like that! What do I know? Who cares? Don't blame me!" In their own ways, Lucy and Sally are a lot like Job in asserting that there are plenty of bad things happening in the world that are really nobody's fault—they just happen, that's all. And the sportswriter is like Job's friends in asserting that life should be fair. At least enough good things ought to happen to offset the bad. Dan Jensen should have gotten *some* kind of medal!

These issues are not easy nor are they comfortable to talk about. It would seem easier, even better, to ignore them or put them out of our minds. But not talking about them leaves us unprepared and overly vulnerable when the inevitable bad things do come our way. It establishes an unhealthy pattern: If bad things do happen to you, don't talk about them. Keep them to yourself. That's part of the reason why we have a book like Job in the Bible, or a play like MacLeish's *J. B.* Indeed, that is part of the reason why Lent is on the church calendar. We need to talk about these issues. To be sure, part of all of us would rather go straight from Christmas to Easter with nothing in between, especially not the cross, but it is a healthy thing that we do not get to do that.

Why then do bad things happen to good people? In the play *J. B.*, there are three answers from J. B.'s friends. For Bildad, it is fate, that's all. It is the capricious hand of fate. This position was echoed in the newspaper: many wondered why most of the best skiers on the U.S. Alpine team were injured and could not compete at the Olympics. Said a U.S. Olympic official, "It's like somebody has a U.S. Alpine ski voodoo doll and keeps sticking pins in it." It's fate, that's what it is, the malevolent hand of fate. It's an ill wind. It's a string of bad luck. But, according to Zophar, another of J. B.'s friends, that's not the answer at all. He knows what it is! "All humans are guilty." As he says to J. B., "Your sin is simple, you were born a human being!" And since all of us are born sinful, it is perfectly understandable that bad things should happen to us. We deserve it. Then there is Eliphaz, who in *J. B.* is a kind of stereotypical psychiatrist. For him, the answer is that we have been overly guilted, so we have become unhealthy prisoners of our own overblown guilt. But in *J. B.*, as in the book of Job itself, these "friends" are all labeled liars by God. Perhaps one could say, somewhat less harshly, that they had each taken a portion of the truth and made it into the whole truth.

In fact, *J. B.*, like the book of Job, is a resounding protest against the idea that bad things happen to good people because they deserve it or because of any other simple explanation. *J. B.*, like Job and like Jesus, was a good, innocent person, and yet he still suffered outrageously. Perhaps then the question Why do bad things happen to good people? is the wrong question. That seems to be the gist of God's answer to Job and to J. B. When God finally appears in the play, as in the Book of Job, God asks:

> Where were you when I laid the foundations of the earth,
> When the morning stars sang together,
> And all the children of God shouted for joy?

And God continues with question after question: "Do you understand creation? Would you, could you, even if I told you?" Then, more in the Book of Job than in *J. B.*, God points to one wild animal after the other—the lion, the raven, the mountain goat, the wild donkey, wild oxen, wild horses, hawks, eagles, the hippopotamus, and crocodiles. God asks, "Do you, could you understand all these different wild animals and their ways and how they got that way?" J. B., like Job, answers no, and in essence says, "I have been asking the wrong question." He does indeed repent, but not of any sin. He is innocent and righteous and has been from the beginning. What he repents of is having asked the wrong question. What then is the right question?

I think that the right question is: What can we do *when* bad things happen to us or to others we know and care about? The answer to this question is not easy either, but we can at least get further with it than with the other. The first clue to its answer comes from Jesus' experience in the wilderness. He had just been baptized, found out that he was God's special child with a special destiny, and yet here he was, driven into the wilderness by the Holy Spirit to be tested by Satan. And, as Mark tells us, his only companions there were Satan, wild beasts, and angels. If I had been in Jesus' shoes (sandals?), I would have been OK with the angels, but Satan and wild beasts I could have done without. And I would have had good reason to think that I might have been spared these latter companions. In Leviticus 26, for example, it says that if you are good, and if you listen to God, you will be spared confrontations with wild beasts. Only if you are bad will you have to face them. And yet here is Jesus, God's special child, fresh out of the womb of his baptism, if you will, in the wilderness with the wild beasts. Why? My hunch is that he had to learn what Job had to learn before him—namely, that the wild beasts teach us that there are things in the world over which no one has control, not us, not God's special child, not, it seems, even God! Freedom and chance are built into the system and cannot be selectively removed. Creation cannot be domesticized.

But what about the other "companions," Satan and the angels? Satan is out there to do what Satan does best, or what that aspect of life symbolized by Satan does best. Satan is like a test-track driver whose purpose it is to test out every car that comes off the assembly line, including the Jesus model. So God's special child was not spared this testing any more than he was spared an untimely and undeserved death on the cross.

But—and this is a very important "but"—he was not left alone to face the wild beasts and Satan out there in the wilderness.

Angels were there as well. They represent the caring presence of God, the promise that God will walk with us no matter what or when, even into the darkest and most shadowed valleys. What do we do when bad things happen to us? When they happen, we are pushed to relearn that love is a permanent option built into life itself. We are not left to walk through these shadowed valleys of life alone. In a sense, that is what the conclusion of *J. B.* affirms. After J. B. has lost everything and his wife Sarah has left him because she could no longer help him, she sees a forsythia bush starting to bloom amid the ashes. Forsythia is a bush that blossoms very early in the spring, a sign of the end of winter. It puts out a shower of yellow petals before its leaves come out. So right on what look like frozen, dead stalks, beautiful, bright, golden signs of new life emerge. It is the sight of this special bush in bloom which pushes Sarah to return to J. B. For her it is a sign of love, not just her love for J. B., but a sign of the love that is built into life itself. As she says to J. B., "You wanted justice, and there was none . . . only love." She affirms this option as she says, "Blow on the coal of the heart, and we'll see; blow on the coal of the heart and we'll know."

So the first part of the answer to the question, What can we do when bad things happen? is to affirm the option (that is always there) of love, of life stronger than death. The second part of the answer is to use the bad things as occasions to grow. Without the testing Jesus faced in the wilderness, I'm not sure how he would have fared against all the other testing that was to come. But since he used it to learn and grow, he could face the many other tests that came his way with wisdom and courage. In the words of Rabbi Kushner, "We do have a lot to say about what suffering does to us, what sort of people we become because of it. Pain makes some people bitter and envious. It makes others sensitive and compassionate." The choice is ours. We can snuff out the coal of the heart and retreat in bitterness, or we can blow on the coal of the heart and let it become the source of new energy to grow in love. We don't seem to get to choose whether bad things will happen, but we do get to choose how we will act and whom we will become when they do.

SIX

Preaching as Storytelling

MICHAEL E. WILLIAMS

> Tell me a story.
>
> In this century, and moment of mania,
> Tell me a story.
>
> Make it a story of great distances, and starlight.
>
> The name of the story will be Time.
> But you must not pronounce its name.
>
> Tell me a story of deep delight.
>
> *—Audubon: A Vision,*
> Robert Penn Warren

My mother's family homeplace had two porches. One faced the back lot, the path to the barn, and the outhouse. The other looked down on a long hill that led to a gravel road across which lay a large field, a line of trees that marked Crockett's Creek, and, barely visible through the trees, the tin roof of Crockett's Creek Baptist Church (founded 1804). This frame structure had housed and nurtured the family of Luke and Neuma Cherry, including children, grandchildren, various aunts, cousins, and people of no special relation to the family but needy of a place to live. I was one of the grandchildren.

If it is true that humans dwell in a house of language, as some philosophers suggest, then this house with its two porches is the home of my imagination and the source of the language in which I continue to dwell. But my initial encounter with the power of words to make a home for us on earth did not take place in a classroom nor did it come from a philosopher. No, its homeplace was a farmhouse porch and its voice was that of a woman in her seventies.

My earliest memories are of sitting on the porch that faced the hill and creek, swinging in a porch swing, listening to my great-aunt tell stories and sing songs. Her name was Minerva Cherry, but we all called her Auntie (pronounced "Ainty"). While the other members of the household did the chores, we sat on the porch, she, who was considered too old to be useful, and I, who was considered too young to be useful. We sat swinging in our uselessness and took part in the truly important activities of life—telling stories and singing songs.

NARRATIVE AND THE PERSONAL:
IDENTITY

The hillside porch (which I called the front porch, though the rest of the family called it the back) was the place where I was told stories that were clearly intended for my benefit. They were offered as gifts, a part of the family legacy. They were my entertainment, and delighted both teller and hearer. They were intended for my edification as well, but were neither explained nor presented in a pedantic fashion. Rather, these offerings of words were carried in memory, then offered like treasures.

The narratives I recall being told on the front porch were all from the oral tradition. The first type of story had members of my family as characters. The most memorable among them is my great-grandfather, George Washington Cherry. Born in the mid-1840s, G. W. Cherry served in the Confederate army during the War between the States. Most of the stories Ainty told me of her father's life came from a time she could not personally have been privy to. They were recollections from his childhood, long before he married or fathered children. These stories were tales told to Ainty by her father or by others among her aunts, uncles, and cousins. She was simply passing them along to me.

She would tell of her father's school days before public education was established in Tennessee. He attended a private academy in the town of Dover some twelve or thirteen miles from the home-place. He had a town family, or school family, with which he lived during the week. This family had several sons, a daughter, and (of all things) a parrot. My great-grandfather and the boys delighted in the fact that the parrot would repeat phrases it heard from members of the family. Whenever they found the opportunity the boys would place the parrot near where their sister received her young men friends. Later, after the courting was finished for the evening, they would coax from the parrot a tender name or a loving phrase that they could repeat much to the sister's dismay the following morning at the breakfast table.

Another favorite George Washington Cherry story recalled a Friday evening when he was returning to the very farmhouse in which I was to live. He had gotten a late start home and decided to take a shortcut through the woods. Suddenly he looked up and saw, above the limb of a shadowy tree, two tiny, yellow lights. As his eyes adjusted to their surroundings he realized that they were the eyes of a "painter," my Ainty's word for panther. Realizing that he was in peril George began to slowly back away from the tree, keeping his eyes fixed on the huge black cat on the limb. As soon as he was distant enough to risk running, my great-grand-father turned and fled, and never took a shortcut through that part of the woods again.

Ainty never explained or moralized, never told me what I should think or do as a result of hearing the stories. But whenever I see a picture of a parrot, I think of that mischievous boy who was my forebear. And whenever I walk through the woods, my eyes search the tree limbs—just in case.

Ainty simply offered the stories as a gift, but with them came a deep and abiding sense of belonging to a family. I came to know who I was as I learned who my people were. It was no surprise when I heard of such forebears as Abraham and Sarah, Jacob and Esau, Ruth and Naomi, along with so many others, that I experienced much the same sense of belonging. These characters who populate the biblical narratives are my people just as surely as Minerva and G. W. Cherry.

In recent years I have become convinced that this sense of belonging to a people is a primary reason that my preaching emphasizes telling the stories of our family members from the Bible. I tell them with little specifically didactic thrust, and I attempt to interpret them through the telling itself, with as little additional explanation as possible. Ainty taught me to trust the story to do its work. In my preaching I hope to honor both the stories and that legacy. Unless we know who our people are, we are left without a household of faith, without the sense of belonging to an ongoing community.

A second type of narrative I heard from Ainty in the front-porch swing concerned the early settlers of that region. Many of these tales do not portray the long hunters in a very favorable fashion. Far more sympathetic are the portrayals of the natives of the area, specifically the Cherokee. Again Ainty did not tell these from personal experience. Rather, she was continuing both the substance and the process of passing along oral narratives that she had inherited. She was relating to me, and so to future generations, what she had heard from our common ancestors.

One of her tales of this type told of a long hunter who built a rough cabin in our region when it served as a hunting ground for both the native peoples and the Europeans who came over from the Carolinas. One night during a terrible snowstorm the long hunter heard a knock at his door, and opened it to find a Cherokee seeking shelter from the storm. I can still hear her inflection as Ainty spoke the hunter's harsh words, "Begone, you Indian Dog!" He then slammed the door, leaving his visitor to risk freezing in the blizzard. Several years later, though, the hunter found himself lost at night in a blinding snowstorm. Seeking shelter he could find only a rotten and partially hollow tree to protect him from the wind and snow. The hunter went to sleep curled up in the hollow of that tree, not knowing whether he would survive the night. When he awoke he found himself in strange surroundings. He looked up and saw the person who had saved his life by pulling him out of the tree and bringing him home—that "Indian dog" he had turned away years before.

Again, Ainty never told me what that story was supposed to mean; she let the story do its own work. But it did not surprise me when I later came to learn that Jesus told a story about the kindness of an outcast, a Samaritan. When I heard of Jesus' other parables turning the world on its ear and shaking up its listeners, I understood somewhere in my heart or gut or wherever we truly hear when a word sinks inside us and resonates our innermost being. I had heard a story like that before.

In my preaching today I include numerous stories other than biblical narratives. I do not choose these just to "warm up the crowd" or to illustrate some philosophical or theological "point." Rather, I attempt to discover those stories that provide a doorway into the world of the biblical text, to touch similar feelings or shatter expectations as the parables often do. Any theological reflection or historical background can be woven into the very fabric of the telling. Stories provide pathways of imagination into the biblical worlds and back into our own. I am convinced that to insist on a propositional statement of a story's meaning would block the pathway for my listeners and keep them from taking the journey and experiencing the world for themselves. Again, Ainty was my teacher in trusting the story, the listener, and God, to do whatever needs to be done with the experience of hearing a story.

A third type of story emerged from Ainty's front-porch tellings which was not located in a specific historical period. Usually the characters had no names or their names were of the typical folktale type, such as "Jack." Many of these stories were sung in a ballad style without accompaniment. Again, they were not learned from sheet music or from a songbook. These stories had not been written down as they passed from mouth to ear, then to Ainty and finally to me. They lived only as they were being told and were kept alive in memory when not being told. To learn them you could not go to a book or library. These stories were rendered up only through the all-too-carnal medium of the human voice and body.

One ballad was a conversation between a mother and her son:

What is that blood upon your coat?
My son, come a'tell it to me.

It is the blood of the little yellow dog,
That went along with me, went along with me.

It is too red for the little yellow dog.
My son, come a'tell it to me.

It is the blood of the little gray mare,
That went along with me, went along with me.

It is too red for the little gray mare.
My son, come a'tell it to me.

It is the blood of my own dear brother,
That went along with me, went along with me.

The son tells the mother that he and his brother went out into a field. There they began to argue, and he killed his brother. The mother laments the fact that she has lost both of her sons, one to death, the other because he will have to leave the country for what he has done. The mother then asks a final question, and receives the answer she fears:

When will you return to me, my son?
My son come a'tell it to me.

When the sun rises in the west, and sets in the east,
And that will never be, that will never be.

I did not realize until years later that the song Ainty sang to me is a version of the Cain and Abel story, told from the point of view of Eve. With the help of a folklorist I discovered that it is also related to a number of other English ballads and likely predates Chaucer. How much earlier it might have existed in Middle English or Anglo-Saxon is unknown because it was transmitted by word of mouth. Indeed, it had come down to Ainty and through her to me without having been written down in the process. Before I had learned to read or seen a television, I had inherited an oral tradition, much like those that preserved the biblical narratives long before they were written down.

That may be one reason why I still do not manuscript sermons before I preach them. Unfortunately lately the lack of manuscript is often taken to mean a lack of preparation. This is a misunderstanding: it simply means a different form of preparation, one in which the sermon is spoken into being rather than being captured and held still in ink on a page. Though I may make copious notes during my exegesis of a passage or to save images and stories that might later appear in the sermon, I prepare the actual sermon by speaking it aloud as I drive, run, or shower. Often this sort of preparation takes as much or even more thought and effort than writing a manuscript. Still, this oral method of preparing the sermon is never complete until it is delivered.

Though I may later create a script based on the spoken event of a sermon, the result is never the same. Not that one is superior to the other. They are simply different. There is an immediacy, a presence, a mutuality in the spoken word, while there is a sense of permanence and of the ability to survive across time and space inherent in writing. One legacy of my family's oral tradition is that for me preaching is always primarily an oral event and only secondarily an outgrowth of a written text.

It was on the front porch of my mother's homeplace that stories were told to me face to face for my enjoyment and the formation of my person. Unbeknownst to me and Ainty, it was also the beginning of my formation as a preacher.

NARRATIVE AND EXPERIENCE

The back porch, the outhouse porch, was a different matter. There was no porch swing on this side of the house. No, this was the work side of the house. From the back porch you could see Uncle Marshall when he drove the ancient Ford tractor in toward the barn from the other end of the back lot. It was on this side of the house that chickens were killed and beagles were gathered for hunting. Here, if you were up early enough, you could embarrass Ainty by catching her returning from emptying her chamber pot (which we called by the graceless name, slop jar).

On the back porch adults did not usually tell stories to children. In fact, when the men and dogs stood around the tractor at the end of the day or jarred the early morning silence with their laughter before hunting, they were careful that the children did not hear the stories they told. A stealthy child might sneak close enough to catch a stray word or phrase, one which often had no place in a young vocabulary.

There would come a time, however, when the back-porch stories would have a place in the lives of us children. Normally, after supper in summer, at the time of day country people called first dark, the adults sat in chairs brought from inside, while my cousin Sandra and I ran across the yard chasing lightning bugs; when darkness or fatigue drove us back to the porch Sandra and I were ushered off to bed by my mother or Aunt Betty as the stories continued. It was a landmark evening when we youngsters were allowed to sit on the edge of the back porch and listen as the adults talked. It meant that we were finally old enough to be allowed to remain and overhear episodes from the family stories. None of these narratives was told directly to us. In fact the presence of young ears was never acknowledged. But bits and pieces of the longer stories were repeated so frequently that even as a child I came to know many by heart.

Unlike the stories that were told to me on the other side of the house, back-porch stories were almost always recollections of someone's direct experience. These stories were not considered the possession of any one teller, though each had certain segments that seemed always to be told by certain people. Usually the characters were relatives or neighbors, many of whom I knew personally. The stories took form in conversation among the brothers, sisters, and cousins, all of whom took part in the impressionistic re-creation of a given narrative.

Only in recent years have I begun to piece together some of the family stories that I overheard on those humid summer nights long ago. I had begun to learn, seemingly by osmosis since no one made the learning explicit, about point of view, characterization, plot, and chronology. Though none of the back-porch tellers would have used those words, they taught them by carefully but unselfconsciously unraveling a strand here and a strand there from a larger fabric whose design I would not discover for years.

The sense of overhearing, which Fred Craddock describes so well, was the primary mode of hearing I learned on that back porch. I learned the power of indirection, since I was not being "preached" to or even spoken to directly. Rather, I was allowed to hear. One of the qualities I hope to achieve in my preaching is that sense that together preacher and listeners are overhearing the conversations that are being whispered or shouted within the biblical texts.

This may be one reason I was puzzled the first time a pastor said to me, "Your story approach is all right as long as the text is a narrative, but you certainly wouldn't use narrative when you preach the Letters of Paul." The assumption underlying that remark has led us astray when preaching on Paul. Too often we act as if the apostle simply sat under a tree one day and decided to write a theological essay. In truth, the letters were Paul's responses to an ongoing story taking place in the particular community to which they were addressed.

Neither we nor our listeners can truly have any notion of what Paul said unless we overhear the story, no matter how fragmentary, into which the letters were inserted. That may mean listening for the specific cultural and historical setting of a letter and weaving it into the sermon. Or we may need to find other stories that pulse with the feeling or shimmer with the meaning that is reflected in a particular passage. These will open the doorway through which the congregation will enter the world of Paul's letter. In either case image and story are primary ways of listening to and re-creating the world of the text.

Perhaps all we can hope for in our study and our preaching is that we will listen intently so we might overhear, even in fragments, the ancient voices of our forebears speaking to each other, in the hope that we might find a word to speak among ourselves in our time.

My family members would not have called themselves storytellers. Yet those who sat and spoke on the two porches of the house in which my imagination was born were my first teachers in the art of oral narrative. This gift has marked my living and my understanding in ways of which I will never fully be aware. My personal understanding of the relationship between preaching and storytelling comes from this early period of my life. For me story is not one preaching technique among many to be picked up in seminary. Stories are not ways to dress up philosophical propositions or illustrate points. Stories are encounters with the strange and wondrous landscape and population of the story world which are evoked by the language of (an)other human presence(s) and are shared by us in imagination. Stories are, finally, sacred encounters that tell us who we are, whose we are, and where we belong. But more than that, they bring us to the very frontier of mystery, of other persons, of the world, of God. They hold us while we peer into the darkness and silence.

PREACHING AS OFFERING

Vladimir: What do they say?
Estragon: They talk about their lives.
Vladimir: To have lived is not enough for them.
Estragon: They have to talk about it.
—*Waiting for Godot*, Samuel Beckett

I was fifteen years old and beginning the eleventh grade at a small country school that could approach a respectable size only by including in its roster of students those from kindergarten through twelfth grade. That year there were two new teachers in the secondary school, a married couple both of whom were recent graduates of the local teachers college.

The couple was named Tidwell. I discovered when I looked at my schedule that she was to be my English teacher, and he would teach my speech class, one of the few electives offered in the rather meager curriculum of that rural southern school. I was delighted.

Since my debut (as the tallest student in the class) as the big goat in a first-grade production of *The Three Billy Goats Gruff*, I had enjoyed taking part in plays. As a seventh-grade project I had even adapted, produced, and directed a production of a Mark Twain short story. Before meeting the Tidwells though, my theatrical efforts had been self-initiated and self-directed. While they were great fun, I knew little of what I was doing.

That enchanted junior year, however, our class attended "real" performances of "real" plays, the sort that one could read in literature texts. For example, we saw Shakespeare's *Taming of the Shrew* with my teachers in the major roles, and Arthur Miller's *Death of a Salesman*, in which Mr. Tidwell portrayed Willie Loman.

That fall the junior play was the Kaufman and Hart comedy, *You*

Can't Take It With You. At fifteen I was chosen to portray a grand-father. I began to learn how to take on another persona, the mask that revealed something of the old man that I will one day be. The learning involved my entire being. I came to observe people with a greater empathy than I had before. I listened more intently, not just with my ears but with my whole body. I heard in memory the voices of older adults from my childhood, some of them long dead. But it was not just a general, older adulthood I was seeking to portray, but a specific grandfather. I wanted to see as he saw, hear as he heard, move as he moved. I sought to experience the world as another individual human being might.

I am afraid that the resulting portrayal fell far short of my hoped-for ideal. But I had caught a glimpse of the world through another's eyes, had watched from a new vantage point as the tired and familiar became strange and fresh. I was touched by the power of language to transform both speaker and hearers.

The following spring that first experience of transformation was confirmed. Mr. Tidwell chose, for the state competition, a play that must have seemed far beyond the reach of high-school students, even those from much more advantaged and sophisticated settings than ours. The play was *Waiting for Godot,* by the expatriate Irish writer Samuel Beckett. Its characters include two tramps who wait by a tree in an otherwise desolate landscape for Godot, Godot's messengers, and the travelers, Pozzo and Lucky. There is little plot in the traditional sense and the lines are terse, their intent anything but obvious. The tramps wait. Godot never comes.

I was chosen to play one of the tramps, Vladimir. This character was nothing like the grandfather I had attempted earlier that year. He was like no one I knew. The references in the script ranged from philosophy to the Bible to the music hall, and were mostly lost on our group of teen players. Vladimir's character challenged me to see not just another point of view on the world; rather, it completely rearranged that world for me.

Beckett's characters, the lost and dispossessed, passing the time in games and conversation at an outpost on the frontier of a world that seemed to be at the end of its rope, held a certain fascination for me. Now I feel sure their appeal was partially related to my own adolescent mixture of melancholy and wonder at a world that in the 1960s seemed to be disintegrating rapidly. At another deeper level, however, the character of Vladimir forced me to come face to face with those who for whatever reason live on the margins, even that person inside me who waited, living on assurances that, it seemed, would never be realized.

I came away from the play knowing, without being able to articulate it as I have just now, that as the tramps talked about their lives, desperately seeking some sort of meaning, so all of our stories, plays, novels, poems, theology, philosophy, and, yes, preaching did much the same toward a similar purpose. Through these forms we talk about our lives and the lives of others in an attempt to put ourselves in touch with something or someone in whose presence we will discover why we and so many others wait.

In the years since that play I have become more convinced that as human beings perhaps the finest service we can perform for others is to listen when they talk about their lives and the lives of those who have waited alongside them, and to share their silence after their stories end.

Before I preach I must listen, not to glean the field for possible sermon material, but simply to listen. When I do speak and attempt to talk about my life or the lives of others, I hope I have learned from the playwrights, poets, and storywriters a way of speaking that respects the mystery residing at the heart of each life.

My teachers have been those around us who regularly attempt to listen and then to embody what they have heard. To learn that in-depth listening, I read novels, poems, and stories, and see plays. I am still an apprentice at the embodiment of the word, but I am an understudy of masters. I will name here two such masters, Mark Twain and Flannery O'Connor.

During my late childhood and early teens I read *The Adventures of Tom Sawyer* and *The Adventures of Huckleberry Finn* at least once each year. There are certain especially vivid days in spring that are still Tom Sawyer days for me. There is a feel of adventure and expectation surrounding such days which still almost sends me in search of a raft.

In college I discovered the stories of Flannery O'Connor, the brutal honesty of whose writing is surpassed only by certain narratives in the Bible. A Catholic in the all-too-Protestant south-eastern United States, O'Connor is able to hear the echoes of grace beneath the grotesque noise of modern life. Her grace often carries a large measure of fear and trembling, with little comfort. If this is so, it is only because her hearing is so acute that it is painful. I shudder to even consider desiring such a gift.

The embodiment of language is my task as a preacher. My aim in uttering such ordinary words about ordinary people is to place our lives in touch with the Source of all that is, whose care is over all. I know of no more appropriate way to approach the One who came to us in the ordinariness of human form, who knows the earthiness of our lusts and longings from the inside out.

THE POWER OF STORY

I have learned that the great storytellers were all highly religious people, believers that God takes care of every human being, each and every animal, and that everything we do, think, and desire is connected with the creator of all things.
—Isaac Bashevis Singer, "Genesis"

During the summer of 1973, just prior to entering seminary, I was living in Maryville, Tennessee, and working as a cast member of an outdoor drama performed each year in the Smoky Mountains. After rehearsal season, my work day shifted to begin at five or five-thirty each evening and end at midnight or after. It was my custom to write in the mornings and spend my afternoons haunting the bookstores and libraries of that tiny East Tennessee town and its Presbyterian college.

One hot July afternoon I wandered into a bookstore, part of a national chain that, though it carried a wide selection of bestsellers and self-help books, rarely had on its shelves anything that would startle or even mildly surprise an interested browser. This particular afternoon I was looking for something "different," though I had little idea in what direction, "subject-wise," that might take me.

The cover of the book first caught my eye. Against a background that was almost entirely white were drawings of men in full beards, wearing black hats and long black coats. They looked for all the world to me as if they were dancing, their arms outstretched and one foot off the ground, as if frozen in a sweep of movement. The title floated above the "dancers' " heads, *Souls on Fire*. The author's name, below it, was Elie Wiesel.

As I stood before the bookshelf, skimming the small paperback volume, I hadn't an inkling of the worlds to which it would introduce me and the manifold ways in which these worlds would change my life. I bought the book and spent the next several days alternately devouring and savoring its contents. I was transported to a world that was at once strange and familiar, the Hasidic communities of eighteenth-century Eastern Europe. These villages could hardly have been further removed from the language and culture of the Appalachian mountains. Yet the feeling of isolation, the sense of living outside the mainstream of a dominant culture, and a keen awareness of the paradoxical nature of human existence in light of the mystery we both called God were strikingly familiar.

In the world of the Hasidim I met characters whose lives seemed as foreign to my experience as their names: Rabbi Israel ben Eliezer—called the Baal Shem Tov—founder of the movement, the Maggid of Mezeritch, and Nahman of Bratslav. I was, like Alice, transported into a "wonderland" in which things became "curiouser and curiouser." Still, for all of the book's· curiousness my own curiosity led me to learn more of the life and times from which the Hasidic flowering of story grew.

Hasidism was a renewal movement within eighteenth-century Judaism, roughly contemporary with the Wesleyan revival in England which spawned my own denomination. The founder of Hasidism, Israel ben Eliezer, was called by those within the movement Baal Shem Tov (one who knows the secret name of God). Those outside Hasidism, many of whom actively opposed the movement, said that Israel ben Eliezer was nothing but a teller of stories to children.

Indeed, the telling of stories was one of the characteristic activities of the Hasidim (the faithful ones). These often poor and uneducated Jews were on fire with a fervent desire for the direct experience of God's presence. When they perceived that their religious practice had become too dry and bookish, the Hasidim infused their worship and study with *nigunim* (wordless tunes), ecstatic dancing, and storytelling. Their stories included those told by the rabbis, as well as those told by followers about their rabbis. Some of the stories were serious, some humorous. Most were considered teaching stories, though they instructed gracefully through indirection and paradox. The tales of the Hasidim combine meaning and mystery in ways that carry the listener beyond expected ways of hearing and seeing the world. Some of the stories even bear a close resemblance to the genre we call the household tale or *Märchen*.

After I arrived at seminary I continued to pursue my interest in the stories of the Hasidim. In addition to other works by Wiesel, there were translations, adaptations, and commentaries on Hasidic storytelling by Martin Buber, Meyer Levin, and Dan Ben-Amos, among others. As reading these stories took on a larger role in my academic study, I was offered an opportunity to allow them to be more fully incorporated into my telling and living.

I was already telling stories for churches, civic clubs, and community groups in the Chicago area, when I began to be invited to Jewish community centers to do programs. Invariably I would be requested to include both "hillbilly" tales (the stories I grew up hearing) and Hasidic tales. At first I hesitated to tell the Jewish stories. It felt presumptuous for me—a *goy* (an "outsider")—to tell these older adults, many of whom were survivors of the Holocaust, their own stories. Though by overhearing these stories from another world and age I had come to love them, I felt hesitant to tell them.

Fortunately the program chairpeople insisted, and the listeners who gathered at the community centers were appreciative. That the stories be told seemed more important than the background of the person telling. Only years later was this supportive experience of the Jewish Community Centers confirmed when a friend, a Jewish teller, encouraged me, saying, "The stories are offered to everyone; they simply came to the world through us."

Since that time the wide range of stories from the Jewish tradition have become a part of my life and preaching. They provide much more than the subject matter for sermons, however. The very person of the *maggid*, the storytelling preacher, has become a primary identity for me, for the *maggid* communicates God's love and concern for people directly through stories. My image of myself as preacher is that of a rabbi, a *maggid*, telling stories that open portals into other worlds for both me and those who listen.

CONCLUSION

I am convinced that a major influence on our preaching is the image of the preacher we carry with us as we prepare and as we stand to preach. That primary persona can be the scholar, the counselor, the moralist, or the motivational speaker, among others. While most of us involve one or more of these roles in any given series of Sundays, there is usually one persona that is primary. For me that preaching persona is the storyteller. Indeed, storytelling has provided my primary self-image throughout my life.

I was not taught that this should be my preaching persona in college or seminary. In fact, there were forces in the seminary that worked against any such self-identification. But there were other forces at work as well in my developing self-image, some from my own distant past and some from another, seemingly distant, world.

My personal image of the preacher began to be formed on those two porches of my mother's homeplace in rural Stewart County, Tennessee. On one porch my imagination was shaped by tales that invited me into a personal and cultural past. They were told to me out of love and concern, so that I would know who I was and whose I was. They taught me that I belonged to a family, a community, a people. I was not alone, caught helpless among the pushes and tugs along the road of history. These things were never said in a straightforward manner, but were shown, embodied in the obliqueness of the telling of tales. The stories I heard did not so much teach me as they surrounded me with a climate in which I learned.

On the other porch I was allowed to listen while relatives and strangers told each other of the persons and events that had formed their lives. I was drawn into a world more strange and various than my child's experience had allowed. This prepared me to overhear and enter the ancient world of Scripture, as well as the worlds of the Hasidim and the other cultures and traditions that have shaped my telling of tales.

On the stage of a small country school, I began to learn the power of embodiment, of the word taking on life and flesh in the person of a speaker. I came to know that the pathway into the lives of others lay in showing them something recognizable, an offering of the joys and pains that reached into the deepest, best-guarded precincts of their lives. When such moments are realized, in theater or preaching, we become companions of the imagination, strengthening each other for the journey. The gifts we have for each other are the touch-taste-feel-smell-sound-image of the world that for a moment was ours.

As a preacher I am a mixture of Appalachian raconteur and *maggid*. My influences are rural and rabbinic, my stories earthy and ethereal. The language is both common and rare; it lures the listeners into unfamiliar worlds and returns them to the familiar surroundings of daily life. The words reach out to touch, to move, to reveal the ordinary people and events of life as the treasures they truly are. This is the road I travel toward an ideal glimpsed only for a fleeting moment and then imperfectly.

In this I trust I am being faithful to another storytelling rabbi, Jesus of Nazareth, and the stories of his embodiment of the love of God which have moved generations to call him Messiah.

Where do I go from here? I have recently come to experience in a fresh and much more resonant way the relationship between my own way of preaching, both what I say and how I say it, and the Jewish tradition of biblical interpretation called *midrash*. While I am certainly no expert on this ancient form of preaching and interpreting Scripture, I am struck by the way it offers a context and form for my own use of narrative in preaching.

Midrashim are stories that comment on and interpret biblical texts. Sometimes they retell the text in different words, or take it in directions that move beyond the parameters of the original words. At other times a midrash might be a story that sheds light on or provides entry into some event in the text.

For years I have tried to distinguish what I do from those who include stories in their sermons with little concern for the stories' relation to the biblical text. In addition, I have tried to suggest that stories have a larger and more important role in preaching than dressing up philosophical or theological "points." Until now I did not have a language to speak in a positive way about my own use of narrative as distinct from other approaches.

My preaching is an attempt to explore and discover a modern form of midrash, of telling stories to interpret biblical texts. Where this exploration will take me I do not know, for I am still on the way.

In truth I am on the way in more ways than one. As I write this I am sitting in the airport in Nashville waiting for a plane to Chicago. For the next two days I will be meeting with pastors and seminarians to speak to them out of my experience of stories and storytelling. What will I tell them?

Will I begin with my recollections of Ainty and the house with two porches? Very likely. Will I speak of Beckett and of the theater, of Twain and O'Connor? Certainly references to them will be made. Will the names of the rabbis and the rich tradition of Jewish storytelling appear in my remarks? Of course! But I will tell them one important thing above all else: stories. At least I will tell them the stories.

How will I know what to say? Are there new words for old tales? Or is it enough to invite them along into the wonderland that a story creates, to walk through a world of enchantment, to learn to care for its people and to take the first halting steps toward speaking its language?

These are enough, I believe, but perhaps not the whole story. Could I say that by listening to the tales of other ages and peoples we may just begin to recollect ancient patterns of remembrance, as a young bird "remembers" to search the cracks and crevices of a limb for food just as all its ancestors have done before? Or might I suggest that such remembering can take us back into a time before there was an alphabet, before hieroglyphics, to witness the birth of language itself?

All this is true, but will it suffice? My task is to tell of a kernel of corn in words that will conjure visions of stalks and tassels. Speech must sting the eyes like beads of sweat that roll off the chin to water the earth. Can I help them smell the thick aroma of sweet corn frying in a black cast-iron skillet, or teach their tongues the grainy delight of cornbread?

Taste and see. That's what I will say.
Look and hear?
Touch and know?

Though hardly adequate, for now these words must be enough. At least I will tell them the stories.

And they will tell each other stories. Stories that hint at the scavenger hunt each of us has made through the world. In which we have found . . .
Ah, but that will be their story.
Listen, I will say between each telling.
Listen to the silence between you
into which your voices dissolve.
Be still and know.
Be still and know.

Hard Times: An Interview with Job

Text: Job 26:7–14

I could see him in the distance as I pulled into the long driveway, an old man in a rocking chair sitting bolt upright in his stiff white collar and bow tie, rocking and looking past me into some dream or distant memory. I sat down in the chair next to him and said, "I hear you've seen hard times."

"Hard times? Hard times, you say? Why I guess everybody's seen hard times."

"But I understand," I said, "that you've seen more than most."

"Maybe so," he told me, "and maybe not. That's not for me to say. Years ago it was, I saw my barns burned, my herds destroyed, my children taken all in a day. A day I will remember all my days. My wife told me to curse God and die, but I felt like I was dead already. Then as if those losses were not enough, I soon found myself sitting on a grate picking at my scabs and sorrows with the sharp edge of a bottle of wine whose brand I would have thought beneath me in earlier, better times. Hard times? I guess I have seen some."

"Did you ever hear why you suffered so?" I asked. "I've heard a tale or two."

"I've heard them, too, and for a long time dismissed them as old folk tales. But as the years have passed, at times I've come to almost change my mind. The tempter baiting God with his 'There is not a one of them faithful' routine. God answering, 'Have you considered my servant, Job? There's not another like him on the earth.' I always liked that part especially. 'Sure he loves you,' says the tempter. 'You give him everything he wants.' Which was not altogether untrue. 'Test him but do not touch him,' says God. Then when that was not enough, it was 'touch him but don't kill him.' That was the unkindest word of all. Those stories make as much sense as any I have heard. There is much foolishness in the world. And little wonder, when people imagine God taken in like a customer at a carnival, taken in by a fast-talking sideshow operator."

There was color in the old man's face, and his eyes took on a strange intensity.

"Speaking of foolishness and unkindness, neither God nor the tempter could hold a candle to my so-called friends. How shall I tell you about them? There I was, sitting on my grate cursing my birth, the warm air feeling good to my scaling skin, when they showed up and sat on their folding chairs in blissful silence for seven days. That was the only kindness they showed me. If they just hadn't opened their mouths.

"The first to speak was Eliphaz, the words oozing out from between his lips like a television preacher. 'You have helped so many others through hard times. Now when things get rough for you, you can't take it. You know that when the going gets tough the tough get going.'

"I wished *he* would get going. Eliphaz went on about some vision he had had. That was about all I could stand to hear, though his sermon continued for what seemed like days.

"When he was finished, I simply said, 'Put what I have done on one side of the scale and what I have suffered on the other. See if the two will balance. No, our days are like those of a migrant worker, good only for the season of our usefulness. Then we are tossed aside like so much rubbish. If my sins were great or if God was kind, I would disappear into oblivion, into the land of the dead where not even God could find me.'

"Then the second sitter, Bildad the Shuhite, spoke. I always loved that joke they tell about him. You know: who is the shortest man in the Bible? Bildad the shoe-height. There was truth to it, too. Why, he was small in more ways than one. All he knew about

God, in fact, all they all knew about God, would fit in a thimble. If the truth were told, their God would fit in a thimble. Well, Bildad was the academic type, the theology professor, you might say. 'Let's look at this situation reasonably,' he said. 'Can a good God cause evil? Can a just God deal unjustly? If we look at the scriptures we will find . . .' That's where I tuned out. It's one thing to quote the Bible in the classroom, and quite another to throw those same words into the face of one who has lost everything. Well, I hadn't lost quite everything; I still had my integrity intact.

"When the professor was finished, I stated my case, 'I know that if a mere mortal were to take the Judge of the universe to court there would hardly be a chance to win the case. All I want is for God to come and present the prosecution's case: that I deserve what I have suffered. I would defend my integrity, in turn. But who could ever hope to win such a trial? I am a runner whose race is almost run. Why was I ever shoved from the blocks, pushed from the womb into such a world?'

"Then Zophar spoke. There was fire in his calm voice, a voice for many causes, in whose heart the fire of justice lived. 'So you have not sinned, you say. I know there was no intentional meanness in you. But can you say that the life you lived did not contribute to the suffering of others—the hungry, homeless, helpless of the world?'

"I heard Zophar out. His words rang with more truth than the other two. Still I answered, 'What you say may well be true for me, but they are just as true for you. Why is it, then, that I sit here in my grief, scraping sores, while you sit with me whole and happy, giving advice? Is that the justice you say you seek?'

"On and on the conversation went until we were joined by a youngster, a student at the seminary, Elihu, come to correct us all. 'You call yourselves teachers, evangelists, and preachers. You can't even correct one poor wretch. The answer is simple . . .' Which is where I stopped listening! Simple answers for me burned with my barns, died with my children, and were scraped away with my scabs.

"Then the breeze picked up, and out of the swirling, whirling wind came the voice of my prosecutor. I got what I had asked for so impatiently. Not an answer, but a trial. 'Stand up,' the voice said to me. 'Get ready for your day in court. I will question you and you will testify. Were you there mixing the mortar when I laid the foundations of the earth? Did you cause the sun to rise this morning or scatter the stars across the sky? Have you visited the house where the rain lives or sat in the homeplace of the snows? Did you set the goats free on the mountains or teach the dog to bark or coax the cat to purr?'

"So on it went, question after question. Before I could frame an answer, another question. I listened. Oh, how I listened! The words washed over me, almost drowning me at times. Finally, when the wind died down, I caught my breath and made my puny plea, 'I know now how much I do not know, that I have spoken out of an endless reservoir of ignorance. I asked for a hearing, and instead I have heard. I demanded understanding, and instead I found mystery. I cried out for justice, and instead I got God. A fair trade for one left with the taste of dust and ashes on his tongue.'

"Then God made the others sacrifice to me. I remember that part with deep and abiding satisfaction. And that is pretty much the way it went, as I recall."

I sat for a time in silence. The only sound was the creak of wooden rockers on the porch floor. The old man seemed settled again, staring into the distance as if he could see the future. I said, "Some say you got it all back, what you had before, that is—even more. Is that true?"

After a time of silent staring he spoke, still peering into the distance. "Oh, that's right. The herds and flocks were as huge and healthy as ever; the barns were as large and well stocked. There are even other children. But was there ever a child who could replace a child? Seven sons and three daughters. Some even suggested that I name them after the ones who were lost, but I couldn't bear that. Children are not sheep or barns to be replaced when they are gone. Now they are grown and I am here. Hard times? I suppose I have seen some hard times, but haven't we all? It's almost time for dinner, would you stay?"

I told him, "No. I have to be at church to be with others who have seen hard times. We'll eat together there."

I crossed the porch toward the car, then turned around. There he sat in his stiff white collar, bow tie, and faraway stare. "I'll tell them what you said," I told him. But he gave no sign of having heard me. Perhaps he was remembering distant echoes of another voice carried to him on the whirlwind long ago.

Selected Bibliography

Browne, Robert E. C. *The Ministry of the Word*. Philadelphia: Fortress Press, 1976.
A classic, linking theology, poetry, and mystery with powerful, practical guidelines for preachers.

Buber, Martin. *Tales of the Hasidim*. New York: Schocken Books, 1948.
A collection of powerful stories from the Hasidic rabbis and a description of the evolution of the Hasidic movement in Judaism.

Buechner, Fredrick. *Telling the Truth: The Gospel as Tragedy, Comedy and Fairy Tale*. San Francisco: Harper & Row, 1977.
Basic introduction to the thought of Buechner—as well as the gospel story—with selections of biblical-narrative retelling which embody what he says.

Craddock, Fred B. *As One Without Authority: Essays on Inductive Preaching*. Enid, Okla.: Phillips University Press, 1971; Nashville: Abingdon Press, 1978.
Perhaps still his most creative work in naming the role of preaching, preparation process, and sermon formation.

———. *Overhearing the Gospel*. Nashville: Abingdon Press, 1978.
Powerful linkage of Kierkegaard's indirect communication to preaching as an art.

———. *Preaching*. Nashville: Abingdon Press, 1985.
Craddock's most comprehensive treatment of sermon formation, particularly as impacted by the biblical text.

Crossan, John Dominic, *The Dark Interval: Towards a Theology of Story*. Niles, Ill.: Argus Communications, 1975.
Crossan believes that story actually creates world, "so that we live as

human beings in, and only in, layers upon layers of interwoven story." He describes five fundamental modes of story with special attention to parable.

Davis, Henry Grady. *Design for Preaching*. Philadelphia: Fortress Press, 1958.
The classic work to which most contemporary writers are indebted—sometimes without knowing it. Particularly important is his understanding of the "generative idea."

Eslinger, Richard L. *A New Hearing*. Nashville: Abingdon Press, 1987.
A quick and fairly accurate look at the thought and practice of Charles Rice, Henry Mitchell, Eugene Lowry, Fred Craddock, and David Buttrick.

Gibble, Kenneth. *The Preacher as Jacob*. Minneapolis: Seabury Press, 1985.
Contains an excellent summary of current trends in the narrative style of preaching, but goes on to look at how the preacher has to change in order to authentically use the narrative style.

Jensen, Richard A. *Telling the Story: Variety and Imagination in Preaching*. Minneapolis: Augsburg Publishing House, 1980.
His description of the relative strengths of three options for preaching (didactic, proclamatory, story) is cued by the title.

Kort, Wesley A. *Narrative Elements and Religious Meaning*. Philadelphia: Fortress Press, 1975.
Although Kort presumes the liberal-arts college context in his relating of theology to the narrative art, the book is instructive for preachers for introduction to narrative elements.

Lane, Beldon C. *Faith and the Magic of Language*. A series of four audio tapes. St. Louis: CBP Press, 1988.
Reflections on the power of biblical narrative, stories from the eastern and Hasidic traditions, and suggestions about the use of metaphorical language in the practice of ministry.

———. *Story Telling: The Enchantment of Theology*. Series of four audio cassette tapes. St. Louis: Bethany Press, 1981.
Outstanding for helping the listener recover the power of story as a vehicle for human transformation.

Lowry, Eugene L. *Doing Time in the Pulpit*. Nashville: Abingdon Press, 1985.
Lowry's theoretical understanding of narrative and its claim toward the shaping of the sermon. He sees the sermon as an event-in-time rather than a spatial event as it has traditionally been conceived.

———. *The Homiletical Plot*. Atlanta: John Knox Press, 1980.
A clear and usable five-step process for the development of narrative sermons.

Mitchell, Henry H. *The Recovery of Preaching*. San Francisco: Harper &

Row, 1977.
The multiple levels of rationality which are needed for preaching, and which can be found in the black homiletical tradition.

Rico, Gabrielle Lusser. *Writing the Natural Way.* Los Angeles: J. P. Tarcher/ Houghton Mifflin, 1983.
Very helpful suggestions for freeing up the imagination and enhancing one's creativity. A useful tool for getting inside a biblical text and finding fresh insights from it.

Robinson, Wayne Bradley. *Questions Are the Answer: Believing Today.* New York: Pilgrim Press, 1980.
Contains useful examples of how to preach in narrative form about doctrinal issues. Includes sermons about God, the human, sin, salvation, the church, the Christ, Scripture, and the Spirit.

————. *The Transforming Power of the Bible.* New York: Pilgrim Press, 1984.
Contains the necessary background and leader's guides for group Bible study, mainly about the life-journey of Jesus from his baptism through the resurrection. While the book was not designed for preachers, it provides the kinds of resources which narrative preachers need in the sermon-preparation process.

Roth, Robert. *Story and Reality.* Grand Rapids: Wm. B. Eerdmans, 1973.
A theological understanding of story which is basic to narrative preaching.

Scholes, Robert, and Robert Kellog. *The Nature of Narrative.* London: Oxford University Press, 1966.
The basic primer for those who want to be introduced to narrative theory.

Steimle, Edmund A., Morris J. Niedenthal, and Charles L. Rice. *Preaching the Story.* Philadelphia: Fortress Press, 1980.
A very helpful presentation of the basic issues in narrative preaching relating to the listener, the preacher, the message, and the liturgical context.

Stollberg, Dietrich. *Predigt Praktisch.* Göttingen: Vandenhoeck & Ruprecht, 1979.
An excellent and succinct summary of the process of sermon preparation and delivery which is useful no matter which form one chooses to use for sermon development. Emphasizes lay participation in sermon preparation and feedback. Has a useful guide for laypeople to use to give effective feedback to the preacher.

Wardlaw, Don M., ed. *Preaching Biblically: Creating Sermons in the Shape of Scripture.* Philadelphia: Westminster Press, 1983.
Helpful examples of a variety of narrative sermons.

Wicker, Brian. *The Story Shaped World.* London: Athlone Press, 1975.
A convincing introduction to the narrative quality of experience.

SELECTED BIBLIOGRAPHY

Wiesel, Elie. *Souls On Fire*. New York: Harper & Row, 1972.
   A summary of the Hasidic movement and samples of the stories of the Hasidic rabbis.
Williams, Michael E. *Friends for Life: A Treasury of Stories for Worship and Other Gatherings*. Nashville: Abingdon Press, 1989.
   Contains the retelling of biblical and other stories about relationships. Good examples of story-form narrative preaching.